Bali

Travel Guide 2024

Your Trusted Travel Partner for a Magical Adventure in 2024

Florence Whitehead

Copyright©2023 Florence Whitehead

All rights reserved. No parts of this book may be reproduced, stored in a retrieval system, or transmitted in any form or by any means, electronic, mechanical photocopy, recording, scanning, or otherwise, without the prior written permission of the copyright owner.

Table of Contents

Introduction 7
   Welcome to Bali 10
   About this Guide 12
   Quick Tips for Travelers 15
   Itinerary 18

Chapter One 23
   Getting to Know Bali 23
   Geography and Climate 23
   Brief History and Culture 25
   Language and local Etiquette 28

Chapter Two 31
   Planning Your Trip 31
   Time to visit 31
   Visa requirement 33
   Budgeting and Currency 35
   Health and Safety Tips 37

Chapter Three 41
   Exploring Bali's Regions 41
   South Bali 41
   Ubud and Central Bali 45
   East Bali 48
   West Bali 52
   North Bali 55

Chapter Four 59
   Must-visit Attractions 59
   Temples and Spiritual Sites 59
   Beaches and Coastal Wonders 63
   Unique Markets and Shopping Spots 67

Natural Wonders and Landscapes 71
Chapter Five..**75**
   Cultural Experiences...75
   Traditional Balinese Dance and Music 75
   Art and Craft Centers 80
   Festivals and Celebrations 84
Chapter Six..**89**
   Outdoor Activities 89
   Surfing and Water Sports 89
   Hiking and Trekking 94
   Diving and Snorkeling 98
   Wildlife and Nature Tours 101
Chapter Seven..**107**
   Culinary Delights 107
   Balinese Cuisine Overview 107
   Must-Try Dishes 112
   Popular Restaurants and Warungs 115
Chapter Eight..**119**
   Accommodation Guide 119
   Luxury Resorts 119
   Boutique Hotels 123
   Budget-friendly Accommodations 127
   Homestays and Villas 131
Chapter Nine...**135**
   Transportation in Bali 135
   Getting Around by Car/Scooter 135
   Public Transportation 138
   Taxis and Ride-Sharing Services 141
Chapter Ten...**145**

Practical Tips for a smooth trip 145
Communication and Internet 145
Local Customs and Etiquette........................ 149
Chapter Eleven..153
Recommended Itineraries 153
One Week in Bali.. 153
Two Weeks or More 156
Chapter Twelve..161
Beyond Bali: Day Trips and Nearby Islands .161
Nusa Penida 161
Gili Islands 164
Lombok 167
Chapter Thirteen.. 171
Staying safe and healthy 171
Emergency information 171
Health Precautions 175
Travel Insurance 179
Conclusion... 183

5

Map of Bali

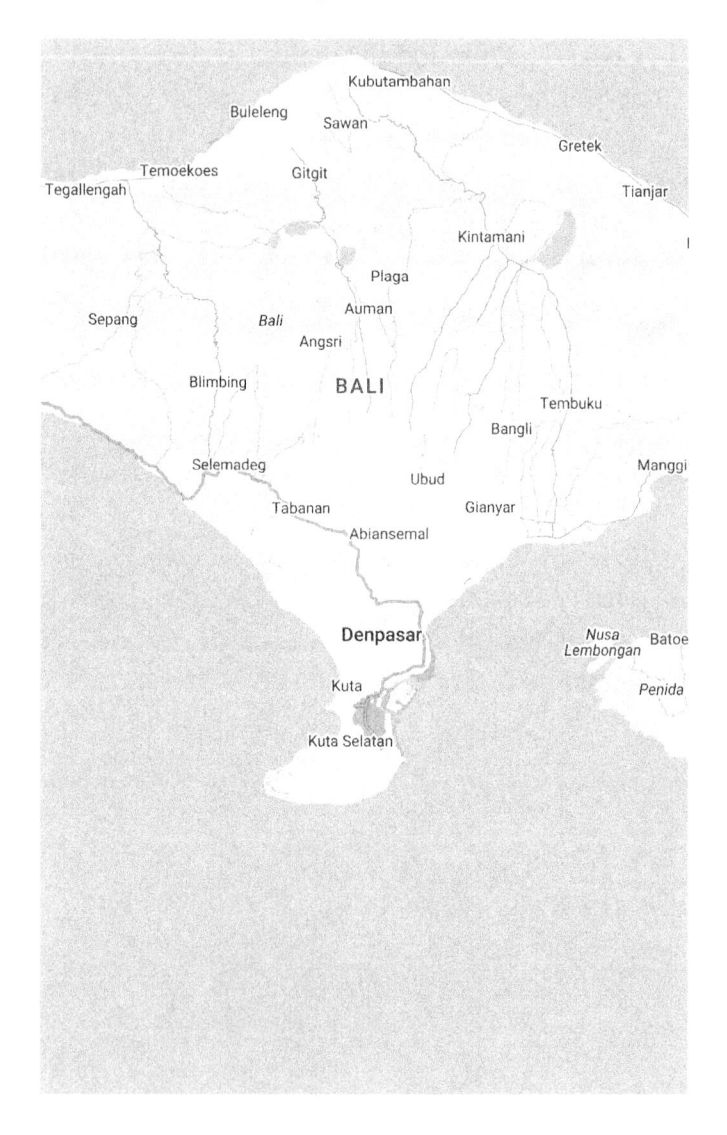

Introduction

As dawn painted the Balinese sky in coral and lavender hues, I stood on the sacred grounds of Bali, a destination that transcends the ordinary. This island of gods, rich in mystique, captivated me from the first breath, carrying the fragrant whispers of frangipani blossoms on the tropical breeze.

In Ubud, the cultural heart, creativity flourished in artisanal boutiques and quaint cafes, creating a vibrant tapestry of colors and local melodies. The Monkey Forest Sanctuary showcased Balis harmonious connection with nature, where mischievous macaques played among ancient temples, offering a spiritual encounter.

Moving beyond Ubud, Balis coastal wonders unfolded with endless golden beaches and dramatic cliffs in Uluwatu, providing front-row seats to breathtaking sunsets. Tanah Lot, with its temple seemingly floating on waves, revealed the spiritual pulse of the island, resonating with tranquility and connection.

Balis allure extends beyond its landscapes to the warmth of its people. Genuine smiles and welcoming gestures made me feel not just as a visitor, but a cherished guest. The locals' stories, shared over Balinese coffee, unveiled a rich tapestry of enduring traditions.

In every moment of my Bali sojourn, from savoring local delicacies to witnessing a Kecak dance, I found bliss woven in the fabric of everyday life. Bali, a sanctuary for the soul, transformed the ordinary into the extraordinary, promising new adventures at every turn.

As my journey reached its final chapter, I realized that Bali is more than a destination; It's a portal to wonder and enchantment. Dear reader, this guidebook is your passport to Bali, a world where each step is a dance, each moment a celebration, and each sunset a promise of a new dawn. Join me in exploring the magic of Bali, where a tapestry of experiences awaits, ready to be woven into the fabric of your unforgettable journey. Come, let us discover the heart of Bali together.

Welcome to Bali

Embark on an extraordinary journey to Bali, an island oasis that weaves together a vibrant tapestry of culture, nature, and genuine hospitality. Nestled in Indonesia, Bali invites you to discover its enchanting landscapes and warm charm.

Step into this tropical haven and be captivated by the vivid hues of Balinese life – lush green rice terraces, intricately adorned temples, and a rich cultural heritage etched in every corner. Bali is a visual spectacle where tales unfold, and the island's deep ties to its heritage are revealed with every glance.

Spirituality permeates the air, evident in the numerous temples and shrines scattered across the landscape. Traditional gamelan music, the aroma of incense, and locals immersed in prayer ceremonies create an atmospheric experience. Bali's spiritual essence extends beyond temples, infusing daily life with tranquility.

In addition to its cultural allure, Bali boasts stunning natural wonders – pristine beaches with golden sands, azure waters, and emerald rice fields. Whether you crave surfing at Kuta Beach or serenity in Ubud's lush forests, Bali caters to all tastes.

Experience the warmth of Balinese hospitality as locals welcome you with genuine smiles. Bali's culinary offerings, ranging from traditional to international cuisines, promise a feast for your taste buds.

In Bali, time slows down, allowing you to savor the magic of the moment. Whether seeking spiritual enlightenment, thrilling adventures, or a tranquil escape, Bali invites you to a memorable journey into the heart of Indonesian Paradise.

About this Guide

Embark on a journey through Bali, where this guide transcends the mundane, serving as your storyteller, confidante, and compass in the land of gods and dreams. Created with a singular purpose, it offers a personal pilgrimage, etching onto its pages the sights, sensations, and rhythms of this tropical paradise.

- A personal Pilgrimage:

More than facts and figures, this guide is my personal narrative. Through my eyes, experience the sunrise over emerald rice terraces, feel the soft sands, and hear the rhythmic heartbeat of Balis vibrant culture. Consider me your fellow adventurer, eager to share every discovery.

- Beyond the Ordinary:

Bali isn't just a destination; It's an immersion in a way of life. This guide captures the essence the spirituality in the air, the creativity in artistic enclaves, and the warmth of strangers turning into friends. Delve beyond the ordinary; this guide is your key to the extraordinary.

- Practical Wisdom, Local Insights:

While Balis magic is in its cultural tapestry, practical wisdom is crucial. Find invaluable tips, insights, and recommendations born from genuine experiences. Consider these pages your treasure trove of local insights, whether navigating Ubud's markets or savoring Balinese cuisine.

- Your Personal Odyssey Awaits:

Envision yourself as the protagonist of your Bali Odyssey. Each chapter unfolds a new facet, inviting you to immerse in beauty, savor flavors, and dance to the rhythm of Bali's soul. Diese Guide is your Ticket to a Journey beyond time and space.

- A Promise of Wonder:

Let this guide be your compass, storyteller, and trusted companion. Whether a first-time traveler or seasoned adventurer, it promises moments of wonder, revelations of beauty, and lingering experiences. As we embark on this literary voyage, may every word be a stepping stone, and every page a portal to Bali's wonders. Let the journey begin.

Quick Tips for Travelers

Certainly! Bali is a well-liked vacation spot because of its stunning beaches, fascinating culture, and exciting nightlife. Here are some quick tips for travelers heading to Bali:

- Respect local Traditions:

Embrace Balinese customs, especially at temples. Dress modestly and be mindful of ceremonies.

- Efficient Transportation:

Opt for scooter rentals for flexibility
Use reliable taxis like Bluebird or Gojek for safe rides.

- Currency and payments:

Carry Indonesian Rupiah (IDR) for small transactions.
In tourist locations, credit cards are routinely accepted.

- **Health Essentials:**
Consume bottled or filtered water.
Guard against the tropical sun with sunscreen and hydration.
- **Art of Bargaining:**
Engage in friendly bargaining at markets and smaller shops.
- **Safety first:**
Exercise caution with personal belongings.
Be mindful of valuables, especially on the beach.
- **Off the Beaten Path:**
Explore local villages and lesser-known beaches for authenticity.
- **Savor Local Flavors:**
Indulge in Balinese cuisine, from Nasi Goreng to Babi Guling.
- **Stay connected:**
Obtain a local SIM card for Internet access.
Wi-Fi is prevalent in hotels and cafes.
- **Learn Local Phrases:**
Basic Indonesian phrases enhance interactions.

- Weather Wisdom:

Plan activities considering the wet and dry seasons.

- Island Etiquette:

Respect homes by removing shoes.
Avoid pointing with your feet.

- Cultural Immersion:

Attend traditional performances or cooking classes.

- Eco-friendly Choices:

Preserve Nature; avoid harming the environment.

- Emergency Preparedness:

Save essential contacts, including Embassy and local emergency services.

Bali's diverse offerings cater to various interests, so customize your journey and relish the island's unique beauty and culture.

Itinerary

Your 5-day Bali itinerary promises a fantastic blend of cultural exploration, island adventures, culinary delights, and serene moments. Travelers are sure to create lasting memories with this well-crafted plan. From vibrant markets to breathtaking landscapes, here's a closer look at each day:

Day 1: Exploring the Cultural Heritage – February 13

- Morning: Badung Market (Pasar Badung), Denpasar: Immerse yourself in the vibrant atmosphere, exploring local produce and handicrafts.

Bali Museum (Museum Negeri Propinsi Bali), Denpasar: Dive into Bali's rich history and art.

- Afternoon: Warung Babi Guling Ibu Oka, Ubud: Savor a delicious lunch featuring the famous suckling pig.

Ubud Waterfall, Rice Terraces & Monkey Forest Private Tour: Experience the natural beauty of waterfalls, rice terraces, and the monkey forest.

- Evening: Locavore, Ubud: Enjoy dinner at a renowned restaurant with a farm-to-table concept.

Devdan Show (Treasure of the Archipelago), Nusa Dua Theatre: Witness a captivating performance of traditional dances and music.

DAY 2: Island Paradise – February 14

- Morning: Bali Nusa Penida All-Inclusive Full-Day Tour: Explore Penida Island, visiting viewpoints like Kelingking Beach and Angel's Billabong.
- Afternoon: Sanur Beach (Pantai Sanur): Relax, stroll along the beach, and enjoy water sports.

The Shady Shack, Sanur: Grab a refreshing snack at this cozy cafe.

- Evening: Uluwatu Temple (Pura Luhur Uluwatu): Witness a mesmerizing sunset and the Kecak Fire Dance.

Jimbaran Beach (Pantai Jimbaran): Savor a seafood dinner on the beach.

DAY 3: Adventure and Relaxation – February 15

- Morning: Ubud ATV Quad Biking Adventure Guided Tour: Experience the thrill of riding through lush landscapes.

Clear Cafe, Ubud: Indulge in a hearty breakfast at this spot known for healthy options.

- Afternoon: USS Liberty Wreck (USAT Liberty), Tulamben: Snorkel or dive to explore the sunken shipwreck and marine life.

Bambu Indah, Ubud: Enjoy a delicious lunch at this unique eco-luxury resort.

- Evening: Potato Head Beach Club, Seminyak: Unwind by the pool with refreshing cocktails.

Metis, Seminyak: Indulge in a sumptuous dinner at this fine dining restaurant.

DAY 4: Nature and Serenity – February 16

- Morning: Bali Sunrise Mount Batur Hike with Breakfast: Hike up Mount Batur for a breathtaking sunrise and enjoy breakfast.
- Afternoon: Jimbaran Fish Market (Pasar Ikan Tradisional Kedonganan): Immerse yourself in the local fishing culture

Sardine, Seminyak: Delight in a seafood feast with a farm-to-table dining experience.

- Evening: Tanah Lot Temple (Pura Tanah Lot): Experience tranquility and witness the iconic sunset.

Bridges Bali, Ubud: Enjoy a romantic dinner with a stunning view.

DAY 5: Culinary Delights – February 17

- Morning: Canggu Grocer, Canggu: Start your day with a delicious breakfast from their wide selection.

- Afternoon: Bali Full-Day Instagram Highlights Tour: Embark on a culinary adventure, sampling Balinese dishes from local food stalls and restaurants.
- Evening: Mozaic, Ubud: Conclude your trip with a memorable dinner, indulging in a multi-course tasting menu showcasing the best of Balinese and international flavors.

Your itinerary captures the essence of Balis diverse offerings, ensuring a well-rounded and unforgettable experience. Travelers are sure to appreciate the careful selection of cultural, adventurous, and culinary experiences.

Chapter One

Getting to Know Bali

Geography and Climate

Explore the captivating island of Bali, an Indonesian gem nestled between Java and Lombok. Spanning 5,780 square kilometers, Bali boasts a diverse geography, featuring volcanic peaks, lush forests, terraced rice paddies, and pristine beaches.

At 3,031 meters, Mount Agung stands as Bali's highest volcanic peak, shaping the island's scenic beauty and fertile soils for agriculture. Journey through the central regions, particularly around Ubud, to witness meticulously crafted rice terraces offering breathtaking panoramic views.

Bali's 550-kilometer-coastline caters to various preferences: from the bustling surf-friendly shores of Kuta to the laid-back luxury of Seminyak. Eastern and northern coasts provide quieter retreats, while the southwestern Bukit

Peninsula offers rugged cliffs and world-class surf breaks.

Experience Bali's tropical climate with distinctly dry (May to September) and wet seasons (October to April). The dry season brings sunny days, ideal for outdoor activities and beach excursions. Despite the wet season's short, intense showers, Bali remains lush and green, maintaining consistent temperatures between 23 to 31 degrees Celsius (73 to 88 degrees Fahrenheit).

Bali's cultural and natural diversity, coupled with its favorable climate, makes it a sought-after destination for travelers seeking adventure, relaxation, and cultural exploration. Whether trekking through volcanic landscapes, exploring ancient temples, or unwinding on sun-kissed beaches, Balis geography and climate create a captivating and ever-inviting environment. Discover the allure of this Indonesian paradise.

Brief History and Culture

Embark on a journey through Bali's rich history and culture, a tapestry woven with resilience, spirituality, and artistic expression. Here's a concise overview:

- History:

Bali's roots trace back to prehistoric times, witnessing early human settlements influenced by maritime trade routes. By the 1st century CE, Hindu-Buddhist influences shaped the Island's religious and cultural identity. In the 14th century, Majapahit's turmoil led to an influx of nobles, priests, and artists, solidifying Hinduism's dominance.

The 19th-century Dutch colonial era brought intermittent conflicts, but failed to suppress Balis distinctive culture. Japanese occupation during World War II and a brief post-war Dutch rule preceded Bali's integration in independent Indonesia in 1949.

- Culture:

Balinese culture thrives on Hindu-Buddhist traditions, promoting harmony with God, nature, and fellow humans. Thousands of temples dot the island, hosting vibrant ceremonies and mystical rituals. „Tri Hita Karana" guides daily life, ensuring a balanced existence.

Arts and crafts hold a global allure, with traditional dances like Barong and Legong, alongside exquisite handicrafts like Batik, ikat textiles, woodcarvings, and silver jewelry. Ubud, Bali's cultural heart, hosts art galleries, museums, and events like the Ubud Writers & Readers Festival and Bali Arts Festival.

Balinese ceremonies, including Galungan and Nyepi, showcase spiritual vibrancy. Galungan signifies the triumph of good over evil, while Nyepi, the Balinese New Year, is a day of silent reflection.

Despite evolving through global interactions, Bali's culture remains rooted in traditions, offering a captivating blend of ancient wisdom and contemporary vibrancy. Explore a world where spirituality, art, and daily life harmoniously coexist in Bali's history and culture.

Language and local Etiquette

Navigate the vibrant culture of Bali with ease by embracing local language and etiquette:

Language:

Officially Bahasa Indonesia, English is widely spoken in tourist hubs. Learn basic phrases like „Selamat pagi" (Good morning) and „Terima kasih" (Thank you) for positive interactions.

Local Etiquette:

Greetings: Offer a warm nod or bow with a smile for a respectful Balinese greeting.

Use of Right Hand: Keep the right hand for gestures and exchanges; The left is associated with personal hygiene.

Temple Etiquette: Dress modestly with covered shoulders, and use sarongs in temples. Maintain silence and respect religious practices.

Removing Shoes: Show respect by removing shoes before entering homes or temples.

Respect for Elders: Use formal language and show deference when interacting with elders.

Public Behavior: Opt for a calm demeanor, avoiding loud behavior in public spaces.

Bartering: Negotiate prices in markets with a friendly and fair attitude.

Offerings: Steer clear of stepping on „canang sari" offerings, acknowledging their religious significance.

Guest Etiquette: Bring a small gift, if invited to someone's home, and embrace punctuality with a relaxed attitude.

Understanding and respecting these Etiquettes not only honor Balinese traditions, but also enrich your experience by fostering positive connections with the welcoming locals.

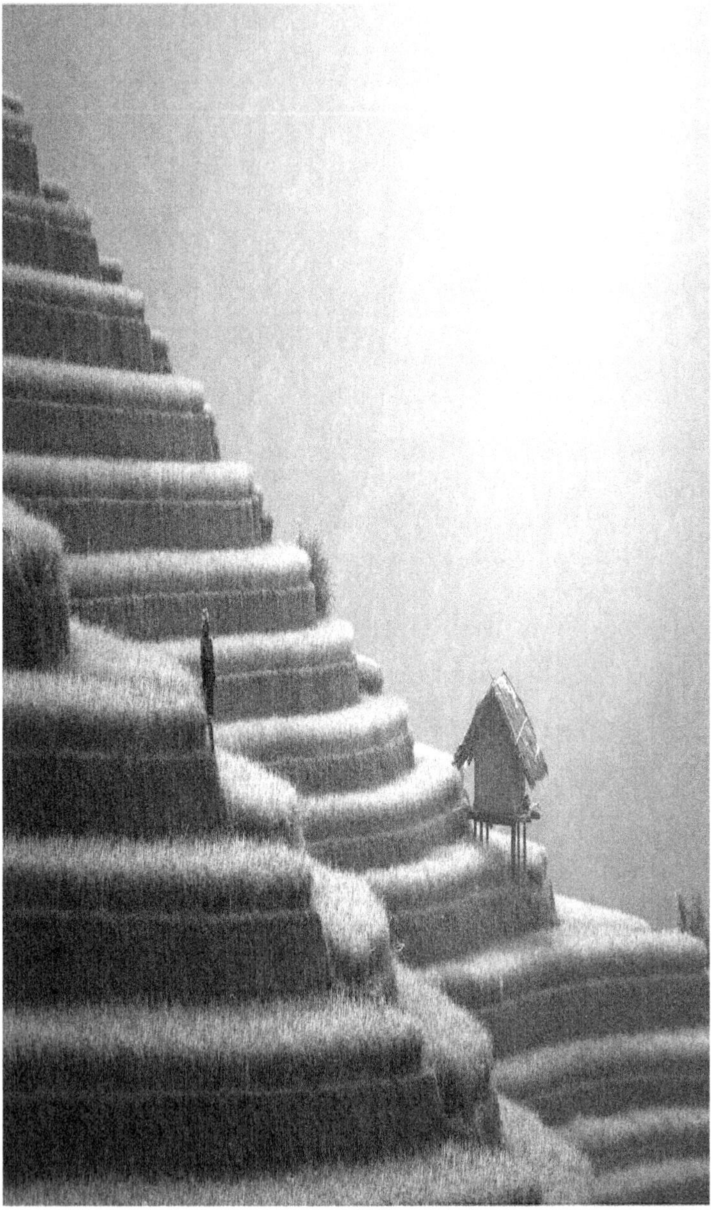

Chapter Two

Planning Your Trip

Time to visit

When to visit Bali depends on your preferences, with two distinct seasons shaping the island's atmosphere.

- Dry Season (May to September):

Considered the best time for many, this season brings sunny days, lower humidity, and minimal rainfall. Ideal for outdoor activities like temple exploration and hiking, though popular tourist areas, especially in the South, can get crowded, particularly in July and August.

- Wet Season (October to April):

Characterized by occasional heavy rainfall and higher humidity, the wet season offers lush green landscapes. Though rain comes in short bursts, this is the low tourist season, providing more affordable accommodations and fewer crowds. Some outdoor activities may be affected, and certain areas can get muddy.

- Shoulder Seasons (April, May, September, October):

Transitional months with a mix of sunny days and brief rain showers, offering a compromise Crowds are lower compared to the peak dry season, making it favorable for those seeking a balance between good weather and fewer tourists.

- Festivals and Events:

Check the Balinese calendar for cultural festivals and events. Nyepi, the Day of Silence, typically in March, offers a unique cultural experience despite the island's temporary shutdown.

Ultimately, the best time to visit Bali aligns with your preferences. Whether you seek vibrant cultural celebrations, water activities, or beach relaxation, Bali accommodates every traveler throughout the year.

Visa requirement

Hier's a concise guide to Visa requirements:

- Visa-free Entry:

Citizens from several countries, including the United States, the United Kingdom, Canada, Australia, and various European nations, could enjoy visa-free entry for short visits of up to 30 days, typically for tourism and social purposes.

- Visa on Arrival (VoA):

For those not eligible for visa-free entry, the Visa on Arrival (VoA) option allows a 30-day stay, extendable for an additional 30 days.

- Social Visa:

Considering a more extended stay? The Social Visa permits an initial 60-day-stay, extendable up to four times, granting an extra 30 days with each extension.

- Multiple Entry Visa:

Planning to leave and return during your stay? Inquire about the Multiple-Entry-Visa option.

- Work and Long-term Stays:

For work or extended stays, explore visa types like Business Visas or Kitas (Limited Stay

Permit), which may involve a more complex application process.

Keep in mind that visa policies are subject to change, and additional requirements may apply. Stay informed by checking with the Indonesian embassy or consulate in your home country or visiting the official website of the Indonesian immigration authorities for the latest updates.

Given the dynamic nature of Visa regulations, it's wise to stay updated closer to your travel date for the most current information. Ensure a seamless journey to Bali by staying informed about the latest visa requirements.

Budgeting and Currency

Navigating Balis budget and currency is key to a well-planned trip.

Here's a concise guide:

Currency:

The official currency is the Indonesian Rupiah (IDR). Use a mix of cash for small buys and cards for larger transactions.

Budgeting:

- Bali caters to varied budgets:

Accommodation: Options range from budget hostels to luxury resorts. Prices vary by location and comfort level.

Food: Warungs and street stalls offer budget-friendly meals, while upscale eateries may be pricier. Dive into diverse Balinese cuisine for cost-effective dining.

Transportation: Scooter rentals are affordable for short trips. Taxis, rideshares, and private drivers are available. Public buses are an option.

Activities: Plan for a mix of free and paid activities, from exploring rice terraces to water sports. Budget accordingly.

Shopping: Balis markets offer crafts and souvenirs. Bargain for the best prices.

- Tips for Finances:

Cash and ATMs: Carry cash for smaller places. ATMs are common in urban areas.

Currency Exchange: Use authorized services for the best rates. Avoid street exchanges.

Tipping: Appreciated but not mandatory. Round up bills or leave 5–10 % in restaurants.

Budgeting Apps: Track expenses with budgeting apps.

- Stay updated:

Check for updates closer to your trip for accurate advice. Currency rates and travel conditions may change. Always stay informed for a seamless Bali experience.

Health and Safety Tips

Prioritizing health and safety is paramount when exploring Bali.

Hier are concrete tips to keep in mind:

- Vaccinations and Health:

Consult your healthcare provider for recommended vaccinations.

Consider hepatitis A and B, typhoid, Japanese encephalitis, and rabies vaccinations.

A basic first aid pack should include all necessary prescriptions.

- Water and Food:

Opt for bottled or purified water.

Exercise caution with street food; ensure it's prepared hygienically.

Wash hands regularly, especially before eating.

- Mosquito Protection:

Use DEET-based insect repellent.

Wear long sleeves and consider a mosquito net, particularly in rural areas.

- Sun Protection:

Use high-SPF-Sunscreen, sunglasses, and a hat to guard against intense Sun.

- Traffic Safety:

Wear helmets when using scooters.

Follow traffic rules and drive defensively.

Be cautious when crossing roads, especially in busy areas.

- COVID-19 Precautions:

Stay updated on COVID-19 guidelines for Bali.

Adhere to local health protocols, including mask-wearing and social distancing.

- Beach Safety:

Be wary of strong currents; swim in designated safe areas.

Stay hydrated, especially during water sports.

- Respect Local Customs:

Honor Balis rich cultural traditions.

Dress modestly at religious sites and ceremonies.

- Emergency Information:

Save local emergency numbers.

Know the location of nearby hospitals.

Consider travel insurance covering medical emergencies.

- Personal Safety:

Secure belongings in crowded areas. Tell someone about your itinerary and trip plans.

Stay informed, practice common-sense precautions, and enjoy Bali while safeguarding your health and well-being. Prior to your trip, check for updates or travel advisories.

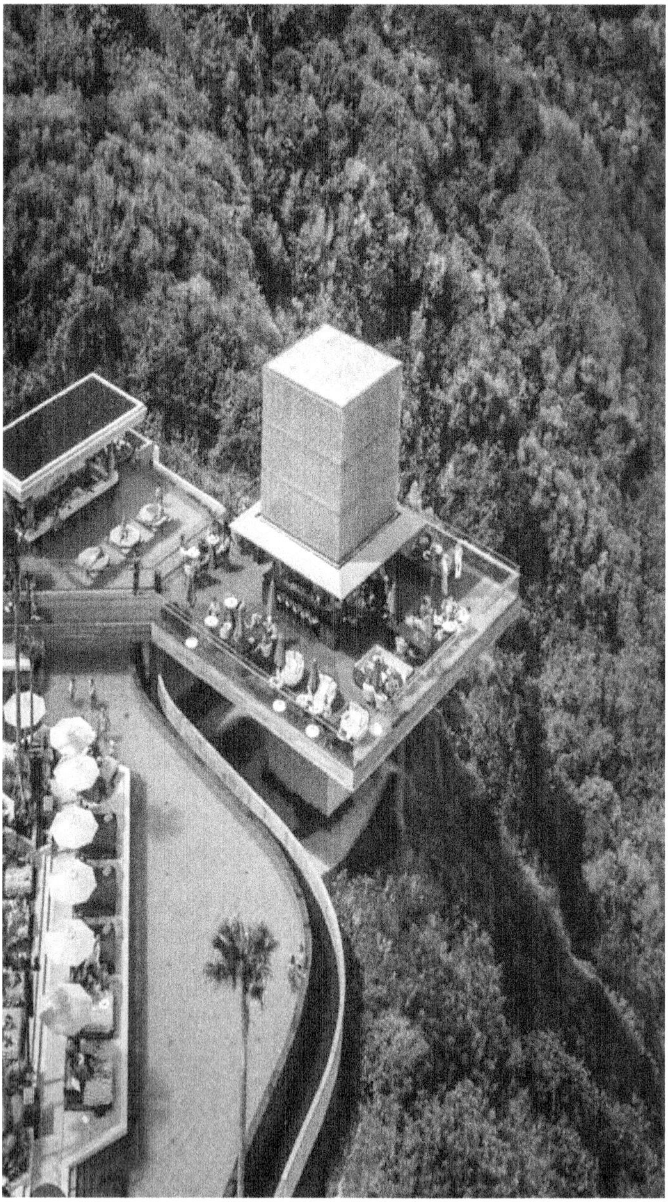

Chapter Three

Exploring Bali's Regions

South Bali

Discover the vibrant allure of South Bali, a region celebrated for its stunning beaches, dynamic nightlife and a myriad of cultural and recreational pursuits. Here are the key highlights:

Kuta:
- Beaches: Kuta Beach, a surfer's haven, boasts a lengthy sandy stretch and captivating sunset views.
- Nightlife: Dive into Kuta's lively scene with bars, clubs, and beach parties

Seminyak:
- Luxury Resorts and Villas: Seminyak stands out for its upscale resorts, boutique hotels, and private villas.
- Shopping: Explore fashionable boutiques, art galleries, and unique shops.

- Dining: Indulge in Seminyak's diverse culinary scene, offering trendy cafes, beachfront restaurants, and fine dining options.

Legian:
- Shopping and Entertainment: Legian offers diverse shopping, from traditional markets to modern malls, along with entertainment venues and live music.

Jimbaran:
- Beach and Seafood: Jimbaran Bay is renowned for beachfront seafood restaurants, providing a picturesque setting for a sunset dinner.
- Luxury Resorts: Experience luxury at resorts with stunning ocean views.

Nusa Dua:
- Luxury Resorts and Golf Courses: Nusa Dua is a resort enclave featuring high-end accommodations, pristine beaches, and world-class golf courses.
- Water Activities: Engage in water sports like snorkeling, diving, and parasailing.

Uluwatu:
- Cliffside Temples: Uluwatu is home to the spectacular clifftop temple, Pura Luhur Uluwatu, offering breathtaking ocean views.
- Surfing: Surfers flock to renowned breaks like Uluwatu and Padang Padang.

Sanur:
- Relaxed Atmosphere: Sanur provides a laid-back atmosphere, calm beaches, and diverse water activities.
- Cycling and Promenade: Explore the beachside Promenade with a rented bicycle.

Canggu:
- Surfing and Bohemian Vibes: Canggu's trendy appeal lies in its surfing beaches, hipster cafes, and laid-back, bohemian atmosphere.
- Rice Fields: Venture into nearby scenic rice fields for a different Bali perspective.

South Bali caters to diverse travelers, from those seeking vibrant nightlife to those desiring a tranquil beach escape. Each area within this dynamic region exudes its own charm and offers unique attractions, making South Bali an exhilarating exploration.

Ubud and Central Bali

Explore the cultural richness and serene landscapes of Ubud and Central Bali:

Ubud:
- Cultural Hub: Considered Bali's cultural heart, Ubud is renowned for art, dance, and traditional crafts.
- Monkey Forest Sanctuary: Home to playful monkeys and ancient temples, this lush forest is a popular attraction.
- Art and Craft Markets: Explore the vibrant Ubud Market for local handicrafts, textiles, and souvenirs.

Tegallalang Rice Terraces:
- Scenic Landscapes: Just a short drive from Ubud, these terraces offer breathtaking views of meticulously sculpted rice paddies.

Goa Gajah (Elephant Cave):
- Historical Site: Explore this ancient archaeological site with elaborate stone carvings, bathing pools, and Hindu statues.

Pura Tirta Empul:
- Holy Water Temple: Visit this sacred water temple for purifying rituals in natural spring pools.

Campuhan Ridge Walk:
- Scenic Walk: Enjoy a leisurely walk with panoramic views of lush hills and rice fields.

Penglipuran Village:
- Traditional Balinese Village: Experience the charm of Penglipuran with its well-preserved Balinese architecture and customs.

Mount Batur:
- Volcanic Views: Consider a sunrise hike for stunning views of the caldera and surroundings.

Tirta Gangga:
- Royal Water Palace: Explore the Water Palace known for its gardens, stone sculptures, and intricate pools.

Gunung Kawi:
- Ancient Temple Complex: This archaeological site features massive stone carvings dedicated to Balinese royalty.

Balinese Dance-Performances:
- Cultural Shows: Attend traditional Balinese dance performances, showcasing intricate movements and colorful costumes.

Ubud Palace (Puri Saren Palace):
- Historical Site: Visit this traditional Balinese palace known for ornate architecture and cultural events.

Ubud and Central Bali offer a tranquil, immersive experience, providing a unique blend of art, spirituality, and connection to Bali's traditions. Ideal for those seeking a different pace and a closer encounter with the Island's rich cultural and natural heritage.

East Bali

Discover the tranquil allure of East Bali, a region celebrated for its natural beauty and cultural richness. Away from the bustling tourist hubs,

Here are some noteworthy highlights:

Besakih Temple:
- Mother Temple of Bali: Nestled on Mount Agung's slopes, Besakih is Bali's largest and holiest temple complex. Immerse yourself in its spiritual significance and savor panoramic views.

Tirta Gangga:
- Royal Water Palace: Once a royal water palace, Tirta Gangga captivates with ornate pools, fountains, and lush gardens. Stroll through this serene retreat.

Tenganan Village:
- Ancient Bali Aga Village: Preserving Bali Aga Culture, Tenganan is among Bali's oldest villages. Explore ancient

traditions and witness traditional weaving.

Candidasa:
- Coastal Retreat: Candidasa offers a serene coastal alternative. Enjoy quiet beaches and explore local markets at your own pace.

AMED:
- Diving and Snorkeling: Dive into Ahmed's underwater wonders, featuring vibrant coral reefs and the USS Liberty shipwreck, making it a haven for enthusiasts.

Taman Ujung Water Palace:
- Historical Water Palace: This former royal retreat boasts beautiful pools, pavilions, and gardens, creating a tranquil and picturesque setting.

Goa Lawah (Bat Cave Temple):
- Hindu Temple: Goa Lawah surrounds a cave filled with bats, offering a unique coastal temple with cultural and spiritual significance.

Bukit Cinta Viewpoint:
- Panoramic Views: Head to Bukit Cinta for breathtaking panoramic views of Mount Agung and the surrounding landscape.

White Sand Beach (Pasir Putih):
- Secluded Beach: White Sand Beach is a pristine stretch with crystal-clear waters, providing a peaceful escape from the crowds.

Mount Agung:
- Volcanic Peak: Challenge yourself with a trek up Mount Agung, Bali's highest volcano, and revel in the breathtaking sunrise views from the summit.

Tirta Sudamala Temple:
- Hidden Gem: Tirta Sudamala, a lesser-known temple with unique black stones, offers a tranquil ambiance for meditation.

East Bali caters to those seeking an off-the-beaten-path experience, blending cultural exploration, natural beauty, and a serene atmosphere. The region invites you to delve into Bali's rich history and spirituality.

West Bali

Discover the tranquil allure of West Bali, a hidden gem offering natural beauty, serene landscapes, and cultural richness. Less touched by tourism, it provides an authentic escape. Here are the highlights:

West Bali National Park:
- Biodiversity: Explore diverse ecosystems, from mangrove forests to coral reefs. Ideal for birdwatching and nature enthusiasts.

Menjangan Island:
- Diving and Snorkeling: Famous for vibrant coral reefs and crystal-clear waters. a paradise for lovers of snorkeling and diving.

Pemuteran:
- Beaches and Coral Restoration: Tranquil beaches and the innovative Biorock Pemuteran project for coral reef restoration.

Gilimanuk:

Gateway to Java: A major ferry port connecting Bali to Java. Experience local life and a starting point for Java exploration.

- Medewi Beach:

Surfing: A surfing destination with long left-hand waves. A laid-back alternative to popular surfing areas in the South.

- Pulaki Temple:

Coastal Temple: Scenic coastal temple with monkeys. Part of a series of sea temples along the north coast.

- Bunut Bolong Tree:

Unique Fig Tree: An iconic tree with a natural hole, considered sacred by the local community. A road passes through it.

- Palasari Village:

Historical Church: Known for its Catholic Church, blending Balinese and European Styles. Reflects Balis religious diversity.

- Sumberkima Village:

Countryside Retreat: Peaceful retreat amidst rice fields and mountains. Experience the rural side of Bali.

- Banyuwedang Hot Springs:

Relaxation: Unwind in natural hot springs surrounded by lush vegetation. A rejuvenating experience.

West Bali beckons those seeking an off-the-beaten-path adventure, offering nature exploration, water activities, and cultural immersion. Ideal for those desiring a quieter and more authentic side of Bali

North Bali

Discover the tranquil beauty of North Bali, a region renowned for its serene beaches and picturesque landscapes.

Here are the highlights:

- Lovina Beach:

Dolphin Watching: Start your day with an early morning dolphin watching experience in Lovina. The calm waters provide an ideal setting to witness these graceful creatures in their natural habitat.

- Singaraja:

Historical Capital: Explore Singaraja, Bali's colonial capital, boasting Dutch colonial architecture, a lively market, and the Gedong Kirtya Historical Library.

- Banjar Hot Springs:

Natural Springs: Immerse yourself in the Banjar Hot Springs, natural hot springs surrounded by lush tropical gardens, believed to have therapeutic properties.

- Gitgit Waterfall:

Scenic Waterfall: Visit Gitgit Waterfall, an easily accessible and stunning cascade surrounded by lush greenery in the Highlands.

- Brahma Vihara Arama (Banjar Buddhist Temple):

Buddhist Temple: Find peace at Brahma Vihara Arama, a Buddhist monastery offering meditation rooms, statues, and intricate architecture.

- Munduk:

Scenic Highlands: Explore Munduk, a charming highland village with trekking trails, lush forests, and breathtaking waterfalls.

- Sekumpul Waterfall:

Trekking Adventure: Embark on a trek through the scenic jungle to reach Sekumpul Waterfall, a cluster of waterfalls offering a mesmerizing natural spectacle.

- Air Panas Banjar (Banjar Hot Springs):

Natural Springs: Experience another set of hot springs at Air Panas Banjar, known for its unique stone-carved spouts releasing warm spring water.

- Aling-Aling Waterfall:

Adventure and Nature: For adventure seekers, Aling-Aling Waterfall provides opportunities for cliff jumping and sliding amidst stunning natural surroundings.

- Buyan and Tamblingan Lakes:

Twin Lakes: Explore the serene Buyan and Tamblingan Lakes, nestled in the caldera of an extinct volcano. Perfect for nature walks and photography.

- Seririt Market:

Local Market Experience: Dive into the authentic Balinese market experience at Seririt Market, where local produce, spices, and traditional crafts await.

North Bali offers a peaceful retreat with a mix of cultural sites, natural wonders, and outdoor adventures. Whether you're into dolphin watching, waterfall exploration, or simply savoring the tranquility, North Bali promises a diverse and rejuvenating experience.

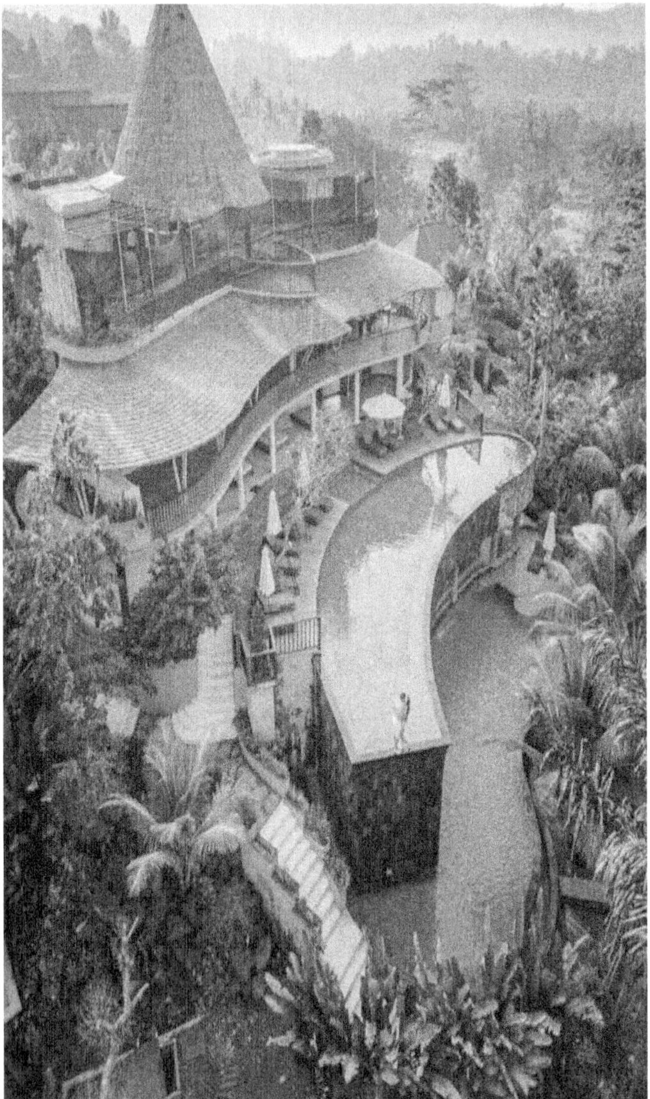

Chapter Four

Must-visit Attractions

Temples and Spiritual Sites

Immerse yourself in Balis profound spiritual heritage by exploring some of its distinguished temples and sacred sites:

Besakih Temple:

Location: Slopes of Mount Agung

Significance: Revered as the Mother Temple of Bali, Besakih is the island's largest and holiest temple complex, a major pilgrimage site featuring multiple temples.

Tanah Lot:

Location: Coastal rock formation near Tabanan

Significance: Tanah Lot, a sea temple perched on a rock, is celebrated for its breathtaking sunset views, making it an iconic and often photographed Balinese gem.

Uluwatu Temple:

Location: Uluwatu Cliff, Southern Bali

Significance: Poised on a dramatic clifftop, Uluwatu Temple offers mesmerizing ocean panoramas and hosts captivating kecak dance performances at sunset.

Tirta Empul Temple:

Location: Tampak Siring

Significance: Tirta Empul, a water temple, is renowned for its sacred spring water, attracting pilgrims seeking ritual purification in its holy springs.

Goa Gajah (Elephant Cave):

Location: Near Ubud

Significance: Goa Gajah boasts an intricately carved cave entrance and holds spiritual and historical importance, dating back to the 9th century.

Ulun Danu Beratan Temple:

Location: Bedugul

Significance: Situated on Lake Bratan, this water temple is dedicated to the lake goddess, offering a picturesque setting that attracts numerous visitors.

Pura Luhur Lempuyang (Lempuyang Temple):

Location: East Bali

Significance: Lempuyang Temple, with its „Gateway to Heaven" (Pura Penataran Agung Lempuyang), presents breathtaking views of Mount Agung.

Pura Taman Ayun:

Location: Mengwi, near Ubud

Significance: Taman Ayun, a royal temple adorned with beautiful gardens and water features, pays homage to the Mengwi Dynasty's ancestors.

Pura Dalem Agung Padangtegal (Monkey Forest Temple):

Location: Ubud Monkey Forest

Significance: Part of the Ubud Monkey Forest Complex, this temple is surrounded by lush jungle inhabited by playful monkeys.

Pura Gunung Kawi:

Location: Tampaksiring

Significance: Gunung Kawi is an ancient temple complex featuring rock-cut shrines dedicated to Balinese royalty.

Tirta Sudamala Temple:

Location: Near Singaraja

Significance: This lesser-known temple, adorned with black stones, provides a serene atmosphere for meditation.

When exploring these sacred sites, don modest attire, including sarongs and sashes, and respect local customs. Follow any guidelines provided at the temples for a meaningful and culturally enriching experience.

Beaches and Coastal Wonders

Discover the allure of Bali's captivating beaches and coastal wonders:

Kuta Beach:

Location: Southern Bali

Features: A lively hotspot with golden sands, renowned surfing waves, and vibrant nightlife.

Seminyak Beach:

Location: Southern Bali, near Kuta

Features: An upscale escape with luxurious resorts, trendy cafes, and a relaxed ambiance.

Nusa Dua Beach:

Location: Southern Bali

Features: A resort haven with pristine white sands, calm waters, and a variety of watersports activities.

Jimbaran Bay:

Location: Southern Bali

Features: Famous for seafood dining by the shore, Jimbaran Bay offers a romantic setting with stunning sunset views.

Pandawa Beach:

Location: Southern Bali

Features: Nestled behind limestone cliffs, Pandawa Beach boasts clear waters, white sands, and breathtaking views.

Dreamland Beach:

Location: Southern Bali

Features: A picturesque retreat with a relaxed vibe, Dreamland Beach is cherished for its surfing waves and coastal beauty.

Balangan Beach:

Location: Southern Bali

Features: Tucked between cliffs, Balangan is a hidden gem offering golden sands and great surf conditions.

Padang Padang Beach:

Location: Southern Bali

Features: A small yet enchanting beach, popular among surfers and known for its appearance in „Eat, Pray, Love."

Nyang Nyang Beach:

Location: Southern Bali

Features: Secluded and pristine, Nyang Nyang Beach is accessible through lush landscapes, offering a tranquil escape.

Lovina Beach:

Location: Northern Bali

Features: Known for black-and-beaches, dolphin-watching, and a laid-back atmosphere.

Amed Beach:

Location: Eastern Bali

Features: A series of fishing villages with volcanic black-sand beaches, ideal for snorkeling and diving.

Menjangan Island:

Location: Western Bali

Features: A small island with crystal-clear waters and vibrant coral reefs, perfect for snorkeling and diving.

Pasir Putih (White Sand Beach):

Location: Eastern Bali

Features: Tranquil Pasir Putih boasts white sands, offering a serene and peaceful retreat.

Secret Beach (Gunung Payung Beach):

Location: Southern Bali

Features: A hidden gem with pristine sands and turquoise waters, providing a secluded escape from the crowds.

Whether seeking vibrant beach scenes, water adventures, or peaceful retreats, Balis coastline promises a diverse array of experiences for every traveler.

Unique Markets and Shopping Spots
Embark on a shopping adventure in Bali, where a plethora of vibrant markets awaits, offering unique local crafts and souvenirs. Here are some of the best:

Ubud Market:
- Location: Ubud, Central Bali
- Features: A bustling market with a wide array of traditional Balinese crafts, textiles, and artwork. Bargaining is a customary part of the experience.

Sukawati Art Market:
- Location: Gianyar, Central Bali
- Features: Renowned for its art and handicrafts, Sukawati Art Market is a treasure trove of paintings, woodcarvings, and traditional Balinese items.

Kuta Art Market:
- Location: Kuta, Southern Bali
- Features: Located near Kuta Beach, this market offers an eclectic mix of sarongs, accessories, and local crafts.

Tegallalang Handicraft Center:
- Location: Tegallalang, Central Bali
- Features: Nestled in the picturesque rice terraces area, this center showcases traditional Balinese crafts, woodcarvings, and handmade goods.

Jatiluwih Green Land Market:
- Location: Jatiluwih, Tabanan
- Features: Adjacent to the famous Jatiluwih Rice Terraces, this market provides local products and souvenirs amidst stunning natural surroundings.

Kumbasari Art Market:
- Location: Denpasar, southern Bali
- Features: A traditional market in Denpasar, offering a variety of goods, including textiles, batiks, and traditional Balinese clothing.

Pasar Badung:
- Location: Denpasar, southern Bali
- Features: Bali's largest traditional market, Pasar Badung, is a bustling hub

for fresh produce, textiles, handicrafts, and souvenirs.

Tanah Lot Night Market:
- Location: Near Tanah Lot, Southern Bali
- Features: A night market providing local snacks, traditional Balinese food, and souvenirs with a stunning view of Tanah Lot Temple.

Sanur Night Market:
- Location: Sanur, southern Bali
- Features: Open in the evenings, Sanur Night Market offers local street food, clothing, and accessories.

Biasa Artspace:
- Location: Seminyak, Southern Bali
- Features: More than a market, Biasa ArtSpace is a gallery and concept store showcasing contemporary art, fashion, and design.

Gianyar Night Market:
- Location: Gianyar, Central Bali
- Features: A bustling night market offering a variety of Balinese street food, snacks, and local dishes.

Kintamani Market:
- Location: Kintamani, Central Bali
- Features: Set against the backdrop of Mount Batur, Kintamani Market is an ideal spot for local produce, spices, and souvenirs.

Tirta Gangga Market:
- Location: Tirta Gangga, Eastern Bali
- Features: A market near the Tirta Gangga Water Palace, offering local crafts, snacks, and souvenirs.

Explore these markets to not only shop for unique items, but also immerse yourself in Balis vibrant and diverse culture. Hone your bargaining skills for a more enjoyable shopping experience.

Natural Wonders and Landscapes

Explore the diverse natural wonders of Bali, each offering a unique and enchanting experience:

Tegallalang Rice Terraces:

Location: Central Bali, near Ubud

Features: Iconic stepped rice terraces, carved in the landscape, providing stunning panoramic views.

Jatiluwih Rice Terraces:

Location: Tabanan, Western Bali

Features: UNESCO World Heritage Site, known for its expansive rice paddies and traditional Subak irrigation system.

Mount Batur:

Location: Northeaster Bali

Features: Active volcano with a challenging trek to the summit, offering breathtaking sunrise views of surrounding landscapes and Lake Batur.

Mount Agung:

Location: Eastern Bali

Features: Bali's highest and holiest mountain, surrounded by clouds, with spiritual significance and trekking opportunities.

Gitgit Waterfall:

Location: Northern Bali

Features: Beautiful waterfall surrounded by lush tropical forests, easily accessible for a refreshing dip.

Sekumpul Waterfall:

Location: Northern Bali

Features: Group of majestic waterfalls surrounded by scenic landscapes, reachable through a trek.

Aling-Aling Waterfall:

Location: Northern Bali

Features: Known for its unique twin waterfall and natural waterslides, a perfect spot for adventure seekers.

Bali Botanic Garden (Kebun Raya Bedugul):

Location: Bedugul, Central Bali

Features: Lush botanical garden with a diverse collection of tropical plants, flowers, and trees.

West Bali National Park:

Location: Northwestern Bali

Features: Home to diverse ecosystems, including mangrove forests, coral reefs, and a variety of wildlife, including the endangered Bali Starling.

Menjangan Island:

Location: Northwestern Bali

Features: Island within the West Bali National Park, known for crystal-clear waters and vibrant coral reefs, ideal for snorkeling and diving.

Angel's Billabong:

Location: Nusa Penida, Southwestern Bali

Features: Natural infinity pool formed in volcanic rock, offering mesmerizing views of the ocean.

Broken Beach (Pasih Uug):

Location: Nusa Penida, Southwestern Bali

Features: Stunning natural bridge over the ocean, creating a unique and picturesque coastal formation.

Crystal Bay:

Location: Nusa Penida, Southwestern Bali

Features: Pristine white, sandy beach with crystal-clear waters, ideal for snorkeling and relaxation.

Melasti Beach:

Location: Southern Bali, near Uluwatu

Features: Scenic beach with towering limestone cliffs and turquoise waters, often less crowded than other popular beaches.

Balis natural wonders cater to diverse preferences, promising adventure, relaxation, and a deep connection with nature for every traveler.

Chapter Five

Cultural Experiences

Traditional Balinese Dance and Music

Immerse yourself in the captivating world of traditional Balinese dance and music, deeply woven into the island's cultural tapestry:

Traditional Balinese Dance:

Barong Dance:
- Description: Depicting the eternal struggle between the mythical lion-like Barong and the evil witch Rangda, this dance is a powerful portrait of good versus evil, often performed during religious ceremonies.

Legong Dance:
- Description: Executed by young girls, Legong is a classical dance known for its intricate movements and expressive gestures. The vibrant costumes add to

the visual allure, making it a staple at temple ceremonies.

Kecak Dance:
- Description: Also called the „Monkey Dance", Kecak involves rhythmic chanting by a large group of men. Scenes from the Ramayana are brought to life in a circle, creating a mesmerizing central storyline

Baris Dance:
- Description: A warrior dance symbolizing the preparation for battle, Baris is performed by male dancers. Strong movements portray discipline and courage in this captivating depiction.

Pendet Dance:
- Description: Pendet is a graceful welcoming dance performed by female dancers during ceremonies. Delicate hand gestures and offerings create a harmonious and inviting atmosphere.

Joged Dance:
- Description: A social dance performed during celebrations. Joged involves a female dancer, inviting audience members to join in the festivities, adding an interactive element to the performance.

Wayang Wong:
- Description: Combining dance, music, and drama, Wayang Wong is a dance-drama narrating stories from the Mahabharata and Ramayana epics. Elaborate costumes and masks enhance the visual spectacle.

Traditional Balinese Music:

Gamelan:
- Description: An ensemble of percussion instruments like metallophones, gongs, drums, and bamboo flutes, Gamelan creates intricate and synchronized sounds, accompanying traditional dances and rituals.

Jegog:
- Description: Utilizing bamboo instruments, Jegog produces deep, resonant tones. Often associated with traditional ceremonies, Jegog Music creates a unique auditory experience.

Gender Wayang:
- Description: A metallophone ensemble played by four musicians. Gender Wayang accompanies Wayang Kulit (shadow puppet) performances, adding a melodic layer to the storytelling.

Beleganjur:
- Description: A marching ensemble used in processions and ceremonies, Beleganjur features drums, cymbals, and gongs, creating rhythmic and dynamic music.

Rindik:
- Description: Played on a bamboo-xylophone-like instrument, Rindik produces soothing sounds, often used for Relaxation and Entertainment.

These traditional dance and music forms are not mere performances, but integral elements of Balinese religious and cultural practices, connecting the community to its rich heritage and spirituality. Attending a live performance promises an enchanting experience of Balinese artistic expression.

Art and Craft Centers

Embark on a journey through Bali's rich artistic heritage by exploring these notable art and craft centers:

Ubud Art Market:
- Location: Ubud, Central Bali
- Features: Vibrant market showcasing traditional Balinese crafts, paintings, textiles, and souvenirs, offering a glimpse into local artistry.

Celuk Village:
- Location: Near Ubud, Central Bali
- Features: Known as the Silver Village, Celuk is renowned for intricate silver and gold jewelry crafted by skilled artisans.

Mas Village:
- Location: Near Ubud, Central Bali
- Features: Home to skilled woodcarvers, Mas Village is a hub for exquisite wooden sculptures and masks.

Batubulan Village:
- Location: Gianyar, Central Bali
- Features: Famous for stone carvings and sculptures, Batubulan showcases the talents of artisans creating intricate statues.

Guwang Art Market:
- Location: Sukawati, Central Bali
- Features: Specializing in Balinese paintings, woodcarvings, and handmade crafts, Guwang Art Market offers a diverse range of artistic creations.

Tohpati Village:
- Location: Gianyar, Central Bali
- Features: Known for batik production, Tohpati Village is a center for traditional Indonesian batik fabrics.

Ubud Royal Palace (Puri Saren Agung):
- Location: Ubud, Central Bali
- Features: Historical site, hosting traditional dance performances and exhibitions of Balinese art and culture.

Threads of life:
- Location: Ubud, Central Bali
- Features: Fair-trade textile gallery promoting traditional Indonesian textiles and supporting sustainable weaving communities.

John Hardys Workshop and Showroom:
- Location: Mambal, near Ubud
- Features: Renowned jewelry brand offering tours of its workshop and showcasing handcrafted jewelry.

Bali Agung Village:
- Location: Peliatan, Ubud
- Features: Cultural village highlighting traditional Balinese life, arts and crafts, with dance performances and workshops.

Five Art Studio:
- Location: Ubud, Central Bali
- Features: Art studio where you can observe and learn traditional Balinese painting techniques from local artists.

Rudana Museum and Rudana Art Gallery:
- Location: Peliatan, Ubud
- Features: Museum and gallery dedicated to Balinese and Indonesian art, boasting a vast collection of paintings and sculptures.

Bali Ceramic Company:
- Location: Ubud, Central Bali
- Features: Studio and gallery specializing in handmade ceramic and pottery pieces, offering insights into the creative process.

These centers not only serve as shopping havens, but also provide a window into the rich artistic traditions of Bali. Whether you seek paintings, sculptures, jewelry, or textiles, each place invites you to appreciate the craftsmanship and creativity of local artisans.

Festivals and Celebrations

Embark on a journey into Bali's vibrant cultural tapestry by participating in these major festivals and celebrations:

Nyepi (Balinese New Year):
- Date: Usually in March
- Features: A day of profound silence, fasting, and meditation, preceded by lively Ogoh-Ogoh parades.

Galungan and Kuningan:
- Date: Occurs every 210 days (twice a year)
- Features: Celebrates the victory of dharma over adharma, with families adorning their homes with penjor and visiting temples.

Saraswati:
- Date: Every six months on the specified Saturday
- Features: Devoted to Saraswati, the Goddess of knowledge and arts, with prayers seeking blessings for wisdom.

Kuta Carnival:
- Date: Annually, usually in October
- Features: A lively Festival in Kuta, showcasing parades, cultural performances, and various competitions, fostering community spirit.

Ubud Writers & Readers Festival:
- Date: Annually, usually in October
- Features: An international literary gathering uniting writers, readers, and thinkers with panel discussions, workshops, and cultural performances

Bali Arts Festival (Pesta Kesenian Bali):
- Date: Annually, June to July
- Features: A month-long celebration highlighting Bali's traditional arts, including dance, music, and crafts, through performances, exhibitions, and competitions.

Bali Spirit Festival:
- Date: Annually, usually in March or April
- Features: A global celebration of yoga, dance, and music, promoting health, wellness, and community with participants from around the world.

Nusa Dua Fiesta:
- Date: Annually, usually in November
- Features: A cultural and arts Festival in Nusa Dua, featuring traditional and contemporary performances, culinary events, and art exhibitions.

Pagerwesi:
- Date: Occurs every 210 days
- Features: A celebration dedicated to fortifying against evil spirits, following Galungan and Kuningan, with prayers and ceremonies.

Tumpek Landep:
- Date: Occurs every 210 days
- Features: A day honoring metal objects, including tools and machinery, with ceremonies to seek blessings for these items.

Immerse yourself in Balis rich culture, witness traditional performances, and experience the strong sense of community during these festive occasions. Each celebration offers a unique insight into Balinese customs and spirituality, creating unforgettable memories for travelers.

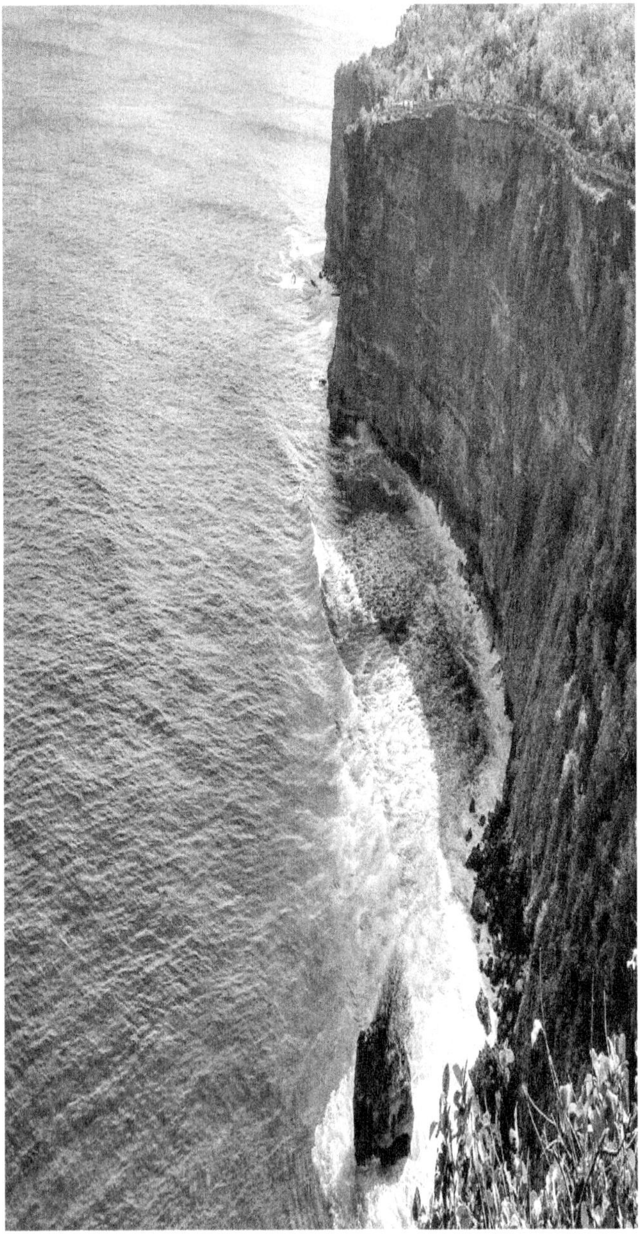

Chapter Six

Outdoor Activities

Surfing and Water Sports

Bali's coastline is indeed a paradise for Surfers and Water-Sport-Enthusiasts. Whether you're a seasoned surfer looking for challenging breaks or someone eager to try water sports, Bali's diverse beaches have something for everyone.

Here's a summary of the best spots for surfing and water activities in Bali:

Surfing Spots:

- Kuta Beach:
    - Suitability: Beginners
    - Features: Consistent waves, surf schools, and a lively atmosphere.
- Seminyak Beach:
    - Suitability: Intermediate to Advanced

- Features: Upscale atmosphere with surf breaks suitable for different skill levels.
- Canggu:
  - Suitability: All skill levels
  - Features: Popular area with various breaks like Berawa, Batu Bolong, and Echo Beach.
- Uluwatu:
  - Suitability: Advanced
  - Features: Famous for challenging waves, including Uluwatu and Padang-Padang-Breaks
- Bingin Beach:
  - Suitability: Experienced
  - Features: Powerful and barreling waves in a picturesque setting with cliffs.
- Dreamland Beach:
  - Suitability: All skill levels

- - Features: Consistent and powerful reefbreak with golden sands.
- Balangan Beach:
  - Suitability: Intermediate to Advanced
  - Features: Long left-hand waves in a scenic location surrounded by cliffs.
- Nusa Dua:
  - Suitability: Water Sports Hub
  - Features: Ideal for jet skiing, parasailing, banana boat rides, and snorkeling.
- Sanur:
  - Suitability: Water Sports
  - Features: Offers windsurfing, kite-surfing and paddleboarding, suitable for beginners.

- Padang Padang:
    - Suitability: Advanced
    - Features: Known for consistent left-hand barrels, gained fame from the movie „Eat, Pray, Love."
- Medewi:
    - Suitability: Longboarding
    - Features: Long and rolling waves on Bali's west coast.
- Serangan Island:
    - Suitability: All skill levels
    - Features: Fun and forgiving waves suitable for surfers of various skill levels.

Water Activities:

- Nusa Dua:
    - Activities: Jet skiing, parasailing, banana boat rides, snorkeling.
- Sanur:
    - Activities: Windsurfing, kitesurfing, paddleboarding.

- Blue Lagoon:
    - Activities: Snorkeling and diving with vibrant coral reefs and diverse marine life.

Bali's coastline caters to a wide range of preferences, making it a haven for those seeking thrilling waves or exciting water adventures. Enjoy the sun, sea, and surf in this tropical paradise.

Hiking and Trekking

Embark on an adventure and explore Balis diverse landscapes through these captivating hiking and trekking destinations:

Mount Batur:
- Location: Northeaster Bali
- Features: A popular sunrise trek with moderate difficulty, offering stunning views of the caldera, Lake Batur, and surrounding landscapes.

Mount Agung:
- Location: Eastern Bali
- Features: Balis highest peak with a challenging trek to the summit, providing spectacular views. Considered a sacred trek.

Campuhan Ridge Walk:
- Location: Ubud, Central Bali
- Features: An easy and accessible trek through scenic landscapes, rice terraces and villages, offering a leisurely experience.

Tegallalang Rice Terraces Trek:
- Location: Central Bali, near Ubud
- Features: Explore the intricate Tegallalang Rice Terraces on foot, enjoying panoramic views and discovering the unique irrigation system.

Munduk to Wanagiri Trek:
- Location: Northern Bali
- Features: A trek through Munduk to Wanagiri, offering views of plantations, waterfalls, and Twin Lakes in a picturesque setting.

Gitgit Waterfall Trek:
- Location: Northern Bali
- Features: A trek leading to Gitgit Waterfall, passing through lush landscapes. The waterfall is a rewarding sight at the end of the trail.

Sekumpul Waterfall Trek:
- Location: Northern Bali
- Features: A challenging trek to Sekumpul Waterfall, known for its

stunning beauty. The trail includes rivercrossings and panoramic views.

Sambangan Secret Garden Trek:
- Location: Northern Bali
- Features: Explore the Sambangan area with a trek through the Secret Garden, discovering waterfalls, springs, and lush greenery.

Aling-Aling Waterfall Trek:
- Location: Northern Bali
- Features: A trek to Aling-Aling Waterfall, known for its twin cascades. Adventure seekers can enjoy cliff jumping and natural slides.

Mount Abang:
- Location: Northeastern Bali
- Features: An off-the-beaten-path trek to Mount Abang, providing stunning views of Mount Batur and Lake Batur with fewer crowds.

Mount Seraya:
- Location: Eastern Bali
- Features: A lesser-known trek to Mount Seraya, offering panoramic views of the surrounding landscapes.

Melanting Waterfall Trek:
- Location: Munduk, northern Bali
- Features: A trek to Melanting Waterfall, hidden in lush jungle surroundings, with scenic landscapes and bamboo forests along the way.

Whether you seek the thrill of a challenging volcano trek or the tranquility of a ridge walk, Balis hiking options cater to diverse preferences and fitness levels. Ensure proper preparation and, if desired, consider hiring a local guide for a more enriching experience.

Diving and Snorkeling

Bali's Premier Diving and Snorkeling Destinations:

Tulamben:
- Diving: Famous USS Liberty Shipwreck, Coral Garden, and Drop-off.

AMED:
- Diving and Snorkeling: Japanese shipwreck, coral gardens; calm waters for snorkeling.

Nusa Penida:
- Diving: Mola Mola and Manta Ray encounters; Crystal Bay and Manta Point.

Menjangan Island:
- Diving and Snorkeling: Stunning coral walls, diverse marine life, clear waters.

Padang Bai:
- Diving and Snorkeling: Blue Lagoon, Tanjung Jepun; Rich corals, diverse species.

Pemuteran:
- Diving and Snorkeling: Biorock Pemuteran Project, Underwater Temple; Calm bay.

Crystal Bay:
- Diving: Clear waters, Mola Mola sightings, beautiful coral reef.

Blue Lagoon:
- Snorkeling and Diving: Calm waters, vibrant marine life; Popular for introductory dives.

Seraya Secrets:
- Diving: Hidden gem near Tulamben; diverse marine life, coral gardens.

Gili Islands:
- Diving and Snorkeling: Gili Trawangan, Gili Air, Gili Meno; Various dive sites, coral gardens.

Secret Bay:
- Diving: Located in Gilimanuk; Known for macrolife, seahorses, unique critters.

Manta Point:
- Diving and Snorkeling: Near Nusa Penida; Famous for resident Manta Rays.

Balis underwater world invites exploration and awe, from historic shipwrecks to encounters with majestic marine life. Whether you're an avid diver or a snorkeling enthusiast, these destinations offer an unforgettable glimpse into the island's vibrant aquatic wonders.

Wildlife and Nature Tours

Explore Bali's diverse wildlife and natural beauty with these captivating tours and experiences:

Bali Bird Park:
- Location: Gianyar, Central Bali
- Highlights: Immerse yourself in a tropical paradise while observing a wide range of bird species, including endangered ones. Engaging birdshows enhance the experience.

Bali Safari and Marine Park:
- Location: Gianyar, Central Bali
- Highlights: Enjoy a safari adventure with close encounters with elephants, lions, and rhinos. The Park also features marine exhibits for a comprehensive wildlife experience.

Bali Butterfly Park:
- Location: Tabanan, Western Bali
- Highlights: Explore a butterfly sanctuary set in a beautiful garden.

Witness various butterfly species in their natural habitat.

Bali Elephant Camp:
- Location: Ubud, Central Bali
- Highlights: Experience an intimate interaction with elephants, including feeding, bathing, and riding. The jungle setting enhances the magical encounter.

Bali Reptile Park:
- Location: Gianyar, Central Bali
- Highlights: Discover the fascinating world of reptiles through diverse exhibits and educational programs. Get up close with snakes, lizards, and crocodiles.

Campuhan Ridge Walk:
- Location: Ubud, Central Bali
- Highlights: Embark on a picturesque trek along Campuhan Ridge, offering breathtaking views of valleys, rice fields, and the Campuhan River.

Bali Green Adventure:
- Location: Various Locations
- Highlights: Engage in eco-friendly adventures like bamboo rafting, cycling through rice terraces, and exploring local villages, promoting sustainable tourism.

Bali Mangrove Tour:
- Location: Various mangrove areas (Sanur, Benoa)
- Highlights: Cruise through mangrove forests, observing diverse bird species and marine life. Some tours may include traditional fisherman's boat races.

Tegenungan Waterfall:
- Location: Gianyar, Central Bali
- Highlights: Experience the beauty of Tegenungan Waterfall, surrounded by lush greenery. Take a swim in natural pools and enjoy the peace.

Alas Harum Agro Tourism:
- Location: Tegallalang, Central Bali
- Highlights: Explore a coffee plantation and agro-tourism site, witnessing the cultivation of coffee, spices, and tropical fruits. Enjoy panoramic views of rice terraces.

West Bali National Park:
- Location: Northwestern Bali
- Highlights: Join a guided tour to explore the diverse ecosystems of the national park, home to various bird species, deer, monkeys, and the endangered Bali Starling.

Bali Botanic Garden:
- Location: Bedugul, Central Bali
- Highlights: Stroll through the botanical gardens, showcasing a vast collection of tropical plants, flowers, and trees from Indonesia and beyond.

Sangeh Monkey Forest:
- Location: Badung, Southern Bali
- Highlights: Visit a less crowded monkey forest, Sangeh, known for its sacred nutmeg tree forest, inhabited by long-tailed macaques.

Whether you seek encounters with exotic animals, scenic landscapes, or eco-friendly adventures, Balis diverse nature tours offer an enchanting blend of wildlife and natural beauty.

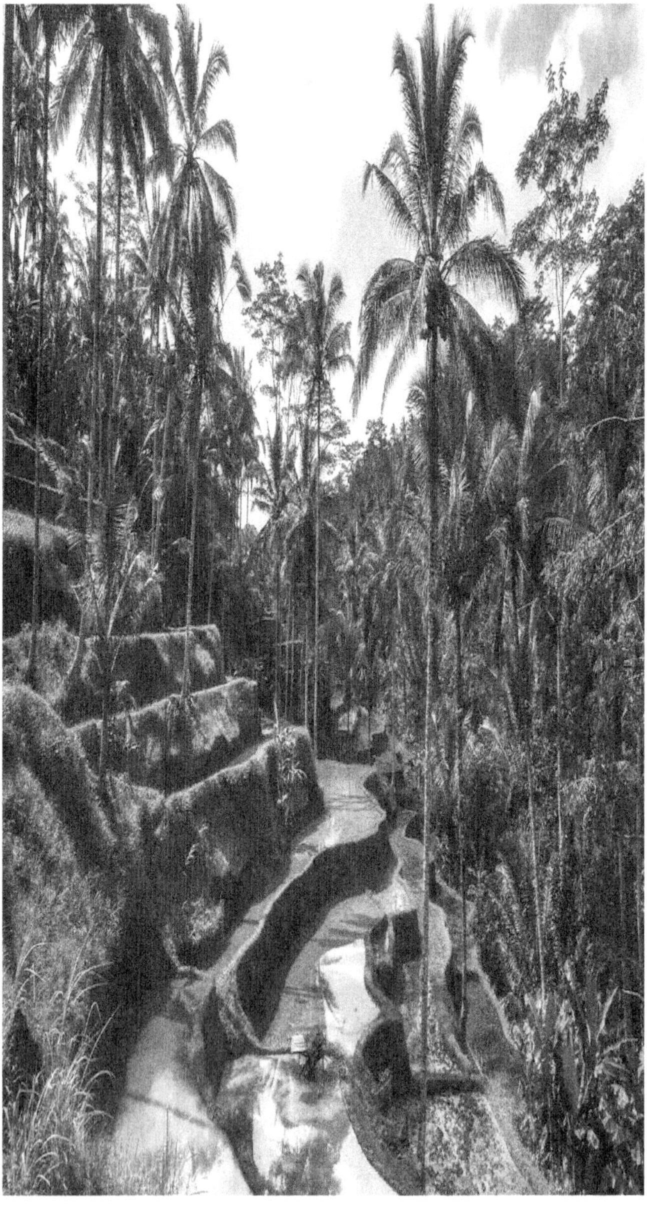

Chapter Seven

Culinary Delights

Balinese Cuisine Overview

Balinese cuisine, with its diverse flavors and cultural influences, is a culinary journey that reflects the island's rich heritage.

Here's a detailed overview of some signature dishes and culinary delights:

Rice as a Staple:

- Subak System: Bali's traditional irrigation system that supports the cultivation of rice paddies. Rice is the staple, often accompanied by various side dishes.

Lawar:

- Signature Dish: A traditional mix of finely chopped meat, vegetables, grated coconut and rich herbs and spices, typically served with rice.

Babi Guling:
- Signature Dish: Balinese-style roasted pork, prepared for special occasions. The whole pig is seasoned, spit-roasted, and served with crispy skin.

Bebek betutu:
- Signature Dish: Slow-cooked dish made with duck stuffed with traditional spices, wrapped in banana leaves, and slow-cooked until tender.

Sate Lilit:
- Signature Dish: A Balinese version of satay, where minced meat (often fish or chicken) is mixed with grated coconut, lime leaves, and spices, wrapped around bamboo sticks, and grilled

Nasi campur:
- Signature Dish: Translates to „mixed rice", featuring rice surrounded by small portions of various side dishes, such as meats, vegetables, peanuts, eggs, and fried-shrimp krupuk.

Lawar Kuwir:
- Signature Dish: A variation of Lawar featuring wild ferns (kuwir) as a primary ingredient, giving the dish a unique flavor.

Pepes Ikan:
- Signature Dish: Fish or seafood seasoned with grated coconut, lime leaves, shallots, garlic, and chili, wrapped in banana leaves, and grilled or steamed.

Jukut Ares:
- Signature Dish: Soup made from the banana tree trunk, flavored with turmeric, lime leaves, and spices, often including meat or fish.

Bubur Sumsum:
- Dessert: A sweet rice porridge made from rice flour, coconut milk, and palm sugar, often served with a drizzle of coconut milk.

Dadar Gulung:
- Dessert: A green pancake roll filled with sweet coconut and palm sugar filling, creating a delightful dessert.

Pisang Rai:
- Dessert: Steamed bananas wrapped in rice flour dough, often flavored with pandan leaves, creating a sweet and chewy delicacy.

Kopi Bali (Balinese Coffee):
- Beverage: Known for its strong flavor, Balinese coffee is often prepared using traditional methods, such as Tubruk (boiling the coffee with sugar).

ARAK:
- Beverage: A traditional Balinese spirit made from distilled rice or palm sap, often used in ceremonies and rituals.

Balinese cuisine celebrates the island's abundant natural resources and cultural diversity, offering a unique and delightful culinary experience for locals and visitors alike.

Each dish tells a story of tradition, flavors, and the vibrant spirit of Bali.

Must-Try Dishes

Bali's diverse culinary scene presents a fusion of influences, showcasing a variety of must-try dishes:

- Nasi Goreng:

Indonesian fried rice, a symphony of flavors with sweet soy sauce, shallots, garlic, tamarind, and optional toppings like eggs, prawns, or chicken.

- Mie Goreng:

Stir-fried Noodles, akin to Nasi Goreng, featuring an array of delicious Toppings.

- Babi Guling:

Balinese-style roast-pork, a succulent ceremonial dish served during special occasions.

- Bebek betutu:

Slow-cooked spiced duck, wrapped in banana leaves, offering rich and aromatic flavors.

- Lawar:

A traditional mix of finely chopped meat, vegetables, coconut and herbs, often enjoyed with rice.

- Sate Lilit:

Balinese Satay, a unique blend of minced fish or meat, coconut, lime leaves, and spices, grilled on bamboo sticks.

- Bebek Bengil (Dirty Duck Diner):

Crispy Duck marinated, deep-fried, and served with flavorful Balinese Sauces.

- Rendang:

Slow-cooked, tender beef immersed in a rich coconut and spice mixture, a Balinese twist on an Indonesian classic.

- Dadar Gulung:

A sweet treat with green pancakes rolled around a delightful coconut and palm sugar filling.

- Bali Coffee:

Experience the bold and rich flavors of Bali Coffee, perfectly complemented by traditional Balinese Sweets.

- Bali Seafood:

Enjoy fresh grilled fish, prawns, and squid at beachside seafood restaurants, a coastal delight.

Explore local markets and eateries to uncover hidden culinary gems. Bali's cuisine is a vibrant tapestry reflecting the island's unique cultural influences, offering a flavorful adventure for every palate.

Popular Restaurants and Warungs

Certainly! Bali offers a diverse range of dining options, from high-end restaurants to local warungs (small eateries).

Here are some popular places to eat in Bali:

Locavore:
- Location: Jalan Dewisita No. 10, Ubud

An innovative and sustainable fine dining spot emphasizing local and organic ingredients for a unique culinary experience.

Potato Head Beach Club:
- Location: Jalan Petitenget No. 51B, Seminyak

A trendy beach club offering diverse cuisines in a stylish and vibrant atmosphere, perfect for a relaxed day by the sea.

Warung Ibu Oka:
- Location: Jalan Suweta, Ubud

Renowned for its authentic Babi Guling (suckling pig), attracting both tourists and locals with delicious Balinese Roast Pork.

Sarong:
- Location: Jalan Petitenget No. 19 X, Kerobokan

A renowned restaurant blending Asian flavors with influences from Indonesian, Thai, Indian and Vietnamese cuisines in a stylish setting.

Naughty Nuri's Warung:
- Location: Jalan Batubelig No. 41, Kerobokan

A casual spot famous for its barbecue-pork-ribs, offering hearty and flavorful meals.

Made's Warung:
- Location: Multiple locations, including Seminyak and Kuta

A long-standing culinary institution in Bali, providing a mix of Indonesian and international dishes for a local dining experience.

Ku de Ta:
- Location: Jalan Kayu Aya No. 9, Seminyak

A beachfront restaurant and lounge with stunning sunset views, known for its cocktails and diverse menu featuring local and international cuisine.

Bambu Restaurant:
- Location: Jalan Petitenget No. 198, Seminyak

A fine dining experience focusing on Indonesian and Balinese flavors, offering rich and flavorful dishes in an elegant setting.

Warung Babi Guling Pak Malen:
- Location: Jalan Sunset Road No. 554, Seminyak

A popular spot for Babi Guling, serving delicious roast pork with various accompaniments.

La Lucciola:
- Location: Jalan Petitenget, Seminyak

A beachfront Italian restaurant with ocean views, offering a romantic setting and a mix of

Mediterranean and Indonesian-inspired dishes.

These selections offer a glimpse into Bali's diverse culinary landscape, but the island is brimming with countless warungs and restaurants catering to all tastes and budgets. Exploring local eateries is a delightful way to uncover the authentic flavors of Balinese cuisine.

Chapter Eight

Accommodation Guide

Luxury Resorts

Bali is home to numerous luxury resorts, offering exquisite accommodations, stunning views, and world-class amenities.

Here are some of the top luxury resorts in Bali:

AYANA Resort and Spa:

- Location: Jalan Karang Mas Sejahtera, Jimbaran

Perched on a clifftop with Indian Ocean views, AYANA boasts a private beach, multiple pools, and the renowned Rock Bar for an unforgettable experience.

Four Seasons Resort Bali at Sayan:

- Location: Sayan, Ubud

Nestled in Ubud's lush jungle, this resort offers spacious villas with private plunge pools, a serene spa, and breathtaking views of the Ayung River.

COMO Uma Ubud:
- Location: Jalan Raya Sanggingan, Ubud

A tranquil retreat in Ubud, COMO Uma focuses on wellness, featuring elegant accommodations and holistic spa experiences.

The St. Regis Bali Resort:
- Location: Kawasan Pariwisata, Nusa Dua

Situated in Nusa Dua, this resort offers opulent villas, a private beach, and exclusive Butler Services for personalized attention.

Mandapa, a Ritz-Carlton Reserve:
- Location: Jalan Kedewatan, Ubud

Along the Ayung River, Mandapa provides spacious villas, a holistic spa, and immersive cultural experiences in the heart of Ubud.

The Mulia, Mulia Resort & Villas:
- Location: Nusa Dua Selatan, Jalan Raya Nusa Dua

An expansive Nusa Dua resort known for elegance, sophistication, and a pristine white sand beach.

Viceroy Bali:
- Location: Jalan Lanahan, Ubud

A boutique retreat in Ubud with stunning valley views, private pool villas, and exceptional dining experiences for a romantic escape.

Bulgari Resort Bali:
- Location: Jalan Goa Lempeh, Uluwatu

Seton Uluwatu's cliffs, Bulgari Resort offers ocean views, luxurious villas, and a private beach, creating an exclusive and serene atmosphere.

Alila Villas Uluwatu:
- Location: Jalan Belimbing Sari, Uluwatu

Blending modern design with Balinese architecture, Alila Villas Uluwatu offers cliff-edge villas, a stunning infinity pool, and personalized service.

Aman Villas at Nusa Dua:
- Location: Jalan Nusa Dua, Nusa Dua

Aman Villas provide a luxurious and serene retreat in Nusa Dua, featuring private villas with plunge pools and access to a private beach club.

These Bali luxury resorts redefine indulgence, offering breathtaking surroundings, lavish accommodations, and impeccable service for an unforgettable experience.

Boutique Hotels

Bali is home to many charming boutique hotels that offer unique accommodations, personalized service, and a distinct ambiance. Here are some boutique hotels in Bali that are worth considering for a more intimate and personalized experience:

The Slow:

- Location: Jalan Pantai Batu Bolong, Canggu

A stylish retreat in Canggu, The Slow seamlessly blends contemporary design with a laid-back atmosphere, featuring art installations, a restaurant, and spacious suites.

Katamama:

- Location: Jalan Petitenget No. 51B, Seminyak

Situated in Seminyak, Katamama celebrates Indonesian craftsmanship and design, offering uniquely decorated suites with handmade furniture and local artwork.

The Artini Resort:
- Location: Jalan Raya Pengosekan, Ubud

Nestled in Ubud's lush surroundings, The Artini Resort charms with traditional Balinese touches, including beautiful gardens and a serene pool.

Tandjung Sari Hotel:
- Location: Jalan Danau Tamblingan No. 41, Sanur

A timeless gem in Sanur, Tandjung Sari Hotel is one of Bali's first boutique hotels, offering a classic Balinese experience in a tropical garden setting.

Amori Villas:
- Location: Banjar Dukuh Kawan, Desa Pejeng Kangin, Ubud

Tranquility and personalized service define Amori Villas in Ubud, with private villas overlooking the Petanu River, creating an intimate retreat.

Bisma Eight:
- Location: Jalan Bisma, Ubud

Bisma Eight in Ubud is a contemporary boutique hotel with modern design, a rooftop bar, and spacious suites offering panoramic views of the surrounding hills.

Uma Karan:
- Location: Jalan Bidadari I No. 9, Seminyak

Uma Karan in Seminyak boasts stylish and cozy rooms, a pool, and proximity to the vibrant dining and shopping scene.

Desa Visesa Ubud:
- Location: Jalan Suweta, Ubud

Offering a village experience, Desa Visesa in Ubud features traditional Balinese architecture, lush rice paddies, and cultural activities.

Cicada Luxury Townhouses:
- Location: Jalan Pura Kayu Putih, Canggu

Cicada Luxury Townhouses in Canggu provide modern and spacious townhouse-style accommodations with a private pool, combining comfort and style.

Villa Kubu:

- Location: Jalan Raya Seminyak, Seminyak

Villa Kubu in Seminyak offers private villas, each with its own pool and garden, providing a secluded and intimate retreat in the bustling area.

These boutique hotels in Bali promise a unique and intimate experience, perfect for travelers seeking personalized services, distinctive design, and memorable stays.

Budget-friendly Accommodations

Bali offers a variety of budget-friendly accommodations, including hostels, guesthouses, and budget-hotels. Here are some options for travelers looking to save on accommodation:

Hostel Ubud:
- Location: Jalan Nyuh Bojog No. 56, Ubud

Nestled in Ubud, Hostel Ubud offers economical dormitory-style lodging with essential amenities for budget-conscious travelers.

Puri Garden Hotel & Hostel:
- Location: Jalan Pengosekan, Ubud

Situated in Ubud, Puri Garden Hotel & Hostel provides budget-friendly options, including hostel dorms and private rooms, complemented by a pool and a laid-back atmosphere.

Capsule Hotel Bali:
- Location: Jalan Patih Jelantik, Kuta

Capsule Hotel Bali, located in Kuta, offers compact and affordable sleeping pods, catering to budget travelers seeking a unique accommodation experience.

Sayang Maha Mertha Hotel:
- Location: Jalan Melasti, Legian

Found in Legian, Sayang Maha Mertha Hotel offers simplicity with budget-friendly rooms, a pool, and proximity to the beach and nightlife.

Kayun Hostel:
- Location: Jalan Legian Kelod No. 181, Legian

A budget-friendly hostel in Legian, Kayun Hostel provides dormitory-style accommodations, communal spaces, and a friendly environment.

POP! Hotel Kuta Beach:
- Location: Jalan Kubu Bene, Kuta

Known for affordability and modernity, Pop! Hotel near Kuta Beach caters to budget travelers with convenient amenities.

Dewi Sri Hotel:
- Location: Jalan Legian, Kuta

Dewi Sri Hotel in Kuta offers budget-friendly rooms, a swimming pool, and a central location for easy access to the beach and entertainment options.

Gora Beach Inn:
- Location: Jalan Pantai Kuta, Kuta

Gora Beach Inn is a simple and budget-friendly guesthouse in Kuta, providing basic accommodations near Kuta Beach.

Warwick Ibah Luxury Villas & Spa:
- Location: Jalan Raya Campuhan, Ubud

Warwick Ibah in Ubud offers a blend of budget-friendly rooms and a picturesque setting along the Campuhan River.

M Hostel:
- Location: Jalan Raya Seminyak, Seminyak

Situated in Seminyak, M Hostel provides affordable dormitory-style lodging with a modern and lively atmosphere.

These budget-friendly options in Bali cater to travelers seeking economical accommodations without compromising on essential comforts. Prices may vary, so it's advisable to check rates and secure bookings in advance for the best deals.

Homestays and Villas

Bali offers a wide range of homestays and villas, providing travelers with comfortable and often more intimate accommodations. Here are some options for homestays and villas in Bali:

Homestays:

- Pondok Vienna Beach Inn:
  - Location: Jalan Pantai Kuta, Kuta Pondok Vienna Beach Inn offers a cozy homestay experience near Kuta Beach, providing simple and affordable rooms with a homely atmosphere.
- Sri Ratih Cottages:
  - Location: Jalan Campuhan, Ubud Located in the serene surroundings of Ubud, Sri Ratih Cottages is a homestay that offers a peaceful retreat with traditional Balinese architecture.

- Lilik House:
  - Location: Jalan Sugriwa, Ubud

Lilik House is a budget-friendly homestay in the heart of Ubud, providing comfortable accommodation with a friendly ambiance.

- Cempaka Belimbing Villas:
  - Location: Jalan Penestanan Kelod, Ubud

Situated in the Penestanan area of Ubud, Cempaka Belimbing Villas is a homestay with villas, offering a tranquil setting surrounded by rice fields.

- Puri Homestay:
  - Location: Jalan Hanoman, Ubud

Centrally located in Ubud, Puri Homestay offers affordable rooms with a garden setting, providing a convenient base for exploring the area.

Villas:

- Villa Kayu Lama:
  - Location: Jalan Raya Kedewatan, Ubud

Villa Kayu Lama provides private villas with a blend of modern comfort and traditional Balinese design, creating a peaceful escape near Ubud.

- Villa Seminyak Estate & Spa:
    - Location: Jalan Baik-Baik, Seminyak

Diese villa complex in Seminyak features private pool villas with spacious living areas, providing easy access to the vibrant Seminyak scene.

- Kubu Manggala Villas:
    - Location: Jalan Sriwedari, Ubud

Kubu Manggala Villas offers private pool villas in Ubud with a focus on privacy and personalized service, creating a serene atmosphere.

- Villa Jerami:
    - Location: Jalan Bali Deli, Seminyak

Villa Jerami offers a collection of private villas in Seminyak with modern amenities, spacious interiors, and a relaxing atmosphere.

- Bidadari Private Villas & Retreat:
  - Location: Jalan Bidadari, Ubud

Nestled in the scenic landscapes of Ubud, Bidadari Private Villas & Retreat offers luxurious villas with private pools and beautiful views.

Balis homestays and villas cater to various preferences, providing travelers with options for a personalized and comfortable stay. Whether you choose the cultural charm of a homestay or the luxury of a private villa, these accommodations contribute to a memorable experience in Bali.

Chapter Nine

Transportation in Bali

Getting Around by Car/Scooter

When renting and navigating vehicles in Bali, whether a car or scooter, is it crucial to prioritize safety and follow local traffic rules. Here's a summary of key tips:

- Renting a Car:

Choose reputable car rental agencies, either international or well-reviewed local companies.

Carry a valid international driver's license or your home country's license.

Get yourself with the laws and ordinances governing traffic in your area.

Utilize GPS-Navigation-Apps, with Google Maps being widely used and reliable.

Be aware of fuel stations, as payments are usually in cash (Indonesian Rupiah).

- Driving Tips:

In Bali, you must drive on the left side of the road.

Exercise caution, especially in densely populated areas

Be mindful of varying road conditions, especially on smaller, less-maintained roads.

Plan for potential traffic, especially in areas like Denpasar and Kuta.

- Renting a Scooter:

Rent from reputable scooter rental shops in tourist areas.

Have a valid international driver's license or your home country's license.

Always wear a helmet, as it is mandatory, and failure to wear one can result in fines.

Familiarize yourself with specific scooter rules and local traffic habits.

Be cautious of road conditions, especially during heavy rain or at night.

- Scooter Riding Tips:

Exercise caution, especially if you're not experienced in scooter riding.

Follow safety guidelines, including helmet usage and adherence to traffic signals.

Purchase petrol from legitimate sources, either small roadside stalls or gas stations.

Park in designated scooter areas, often available at tourist attractions and accommodations.

Consider hiring a local driver if you are not comfortable driving in Bali.

- General Safety:

Stay alert and aware of your surroundings.

Respect local traffic habits and road conditions.

If unsure or uncomfortable driving, hire a local driver for a more relaxed experience.

By prioritizing safety, following local rules, and using common sense, you can enjoy the flexibility and freedom of exploring Bali at your own pace.

Public Transportation

While Bali doesn't have an extensive public transportation system, there are several options available for getting around without renting a car or scooter.

Here's an overview of public transportation modes in Bali:

- Bemos:

Small vans or minivans operating on fixed routes.

Budget-friendly but may not be as comfortable or convenient.

- Public Buses:

Limited coverage, primarily between major towns and tourist destinations.

Schedules may not always be reliable.

- Kura-Kura Bus:

Shuttle-bus service covering popular tourist areas like Kuta, Seminyak, Legian, and Ubud.

Convenient and affordable for traveling between key attractions.

- Taxi:

Widely available, especially in tourist areas.

Use reputable taxi companies, ensure the meter is used, or agree on a fare before the journey.

- Online Ride-Hailing:

Services like Grab and Gojek operate in Bali, offering car and scooter rides.

Convenient and often cost-effective with the option to book through mobile apps.

- Motorbike Taxis (Ojek):

Quick and flexible way to navigate through traffic.

Ojek Drivers can be found at popular spots and street corners.

- Car Rentals with Drivers:

Common practice, providing the convenience of a local guide.

Ideal for avoiding the stress of driving in Balis traffic.

- Cidomo (Horse-Drawn Carriage):

Found in certain areas, such as the Gili Islands and some parts of Bali.

Used for short distances, offering a unique local transportation experience.

- Tips for Public Transportation:

Plan routes and consider alternative modes of transportation to avoid delays.

Always negotiate or confirm fares before using public transportation, to prevent Misunderstandings.

Keep in mind that Bali's traffic conditions can be challenging, particularly in busy areas. Choosing the right transportation option depends on your preferences, budget, and the locations you plan to visit.

Taxis and Ride-Sharing Services

Taxis and ride-sharing services provide convenient transportation options for navigating Bali.

Hier's an overview of taxis and popular ride-sharing services on the island:

Taxis:

- Blue Bird Taxis:

Reputable and reliable Taxi Company.

Recognized by its blue cars with the bird logo.

Use meters for transparent and fair pricing.

Available through the Blue Bird App or hailed on the Street.

- Express Taxis:

Other Taxi companies like Bali Taxi and Ngurah Rai Taxi operate in Bali.

Blue Bird is often recommended for reliability, but competitive rates may be offered by other companies.

Always insist on using the meter for fair fares.

- Metered Fares:

Ensure the use of the meter when taking a taxi for fair pricing.

If a driver refuses to use the meter, consider finding another taxi.

- Airport Taxis:

Official airport taxis are available at designated stands.

These taxis use meters, and the fare depends on the destination.

Avoid accepting rides from tots inside the airport.

Ride-Sharing Services:

- Grab:

Popular ride-sharing app in Bali.

Offers GrabCar for cars, GrabBike for motorbikes, and GrabCar Plus for upgraded rides.

Payments can be made in cash or through the app.

- Gojek:

Widely used ride-sharing-app.

Provides various services, including GoCar for cars, GoRide for motorbikes, and GoCar Plus for upgraded rides.

Payments can be made in cash or through the app.

Tips for Using Taxis and Ride-Sharing Services:

- Use reputable services:

Stick to well-known taxi companies like Blue Bird or established ride-sharing apps like Grab and Gojek.

- Confirm Fare:

For Taxis, confirm with the driver that they will use the meter before starting the ride.

Ride-sharing apps usually display the calculated fare in the app.

- Cash Payments:

Carry Indonesian Rupiah for cash payments, especially if using taxis or negotiating with drivers.

- Pick-up locations:

Use designated pick-up locations when using ride-sharing apps to avoid issues with local authorities.

- Know Your Destination:

Have the address or location of your destination written down or saved on your phone to show the driver, especially in case of a language barrier.

Taxis and ride-sharing services offer a convenient and efficient way to explore Bali, providing comfortable transportation options without the need to drive in the island's traffic.

Chapter Ten

Practical Tips for a smooth trip

Communication and Internet

Communication and staying connected in Bali:

- Internet Access:

Wi-Fi is widely available in accommodations, cafes, and restaurants.

Tourist hubs like Kuta, Seminyak, Ubud, and Canggu have extensive Wi-Fi coverage.

Many hotels and villas offer complimentary Wi-Fi for guests.

- Local SIM Cards:

Purchase a local SIM card for on-the-go connectivity.

Find SIM-card-providers at the airport, in convenience-stores, or mobile-phone-shops.

Popular providers include Telkomsel, XL Axiata, and Indosat Ooredoo.

Ensure your phone is unlocked before buying a local SIM card.

- Mobile Data:

Bali has good 4G coverage in most areas.

Use mobile data for navigation, social media, and staying connected.

- Internet Cafes:

While less common, Internet Cafés still exist in certain areas.

They offer computer rental services and Internet access.

- Communication Apps:

Use messaging apps like WhatsApp, Telegram, and Facebook Messenger.

Useful for staying in touch with friends, family, and fellow travelers.

- Local Calls:

Make local calls with your mobile phone and a local SIM card.

Ensure you have the correct area code when dialing local numbers.

- Emergency Services:

The emergency number in Indonesia is 112.

Know the local emergency services number and save it in your phone.

- Language:

Bahasa Indonesia is the official language.

English is widely spoken in tourist areas.

Learning basic Bahasa phrases enhances interactions with locals.

- Internet Speed:

Internet speed is generally good, especially in popular tourist destinations.

Speed may vary in more remote areas.

- Virtual Private Networks (VPNs):

Consider using a VPN for added security on public Wi-Fi.

Some websites and services may be restricted in Indonesia.

- Time Zone:

Bali follows Central Indonesian Time (WITA), UTC+8.

Be mindful of the time difference when communicating globally.

In summary, Bali offers convenient connectivity with widespread Internet access, mobile data options, and easily available SIM cards. Whether using communication apps, making local calls, or accessing the internet, Balis infrastructure caters to the needs of both tourists and locals.

Local Customs and Etiquette

Understanding and respecting local customs and etiquette is crucial when visiting Bali. Here are some key tips to keep in mind:

- Greetings:

Use the traditional Balinese greeting „Om Swastiastu" with a prayer-like gesture.

When delivering or receiving anything, use both hands.

- Temples and Religious Sites:

Dress modestly when visiting temples, covering shoulders and knees.

Sarongs are often required and available for rent.

Follow signs and rules and avoid walking in front of people praying.

- Sacred Objects:

Do not touch or disturb sacred objects, offerings, or temple-structures.

Maintain a reasonable distance and avoid unnecessary noise.

- Public Displays of Affection:

Keep physical expressions of affection private.

Be mindful of local norms regarding public displays of affection.

- Shoes:

Remove shoes before entering homes, temples, shops, or restaurants.

Leaving footwear outside is a sign of respect.

- Respect for Elders:

Use proper titles like „Bapak" and „Ibu" when addressing elders.

Show respect to older individuals and those of higher status.

- Pointing:

Refrain from pointing, especially when pointing at individuals.

Use your thumb with your fingers folded in when indicating.

- Offerings:

Avoid stepping on traditional offerings (canang sari) on the ground.

- Dress modestly:

Dress modestly outside of beach areas.

Bikinis and Swimwear may not be appropriate in towns or at temples.

- Balinese Calendar:

Be aware of ceremonies and festivals throughout the year.

Some attractions or services may be limited during these times.

- Haggling:

Haggling is common in markets, but do it with respect and a friendly attitude.

- Photography:

Ask for permission before taking someone's photo.

Respect privacy, especially in rural or remote areas.

By being mindful of these customs and etiquette, you'll contribute to a positive cultural exchange and enhance your experience in Bali. Respect for local traditions fosters a more meaningful connection with the community.

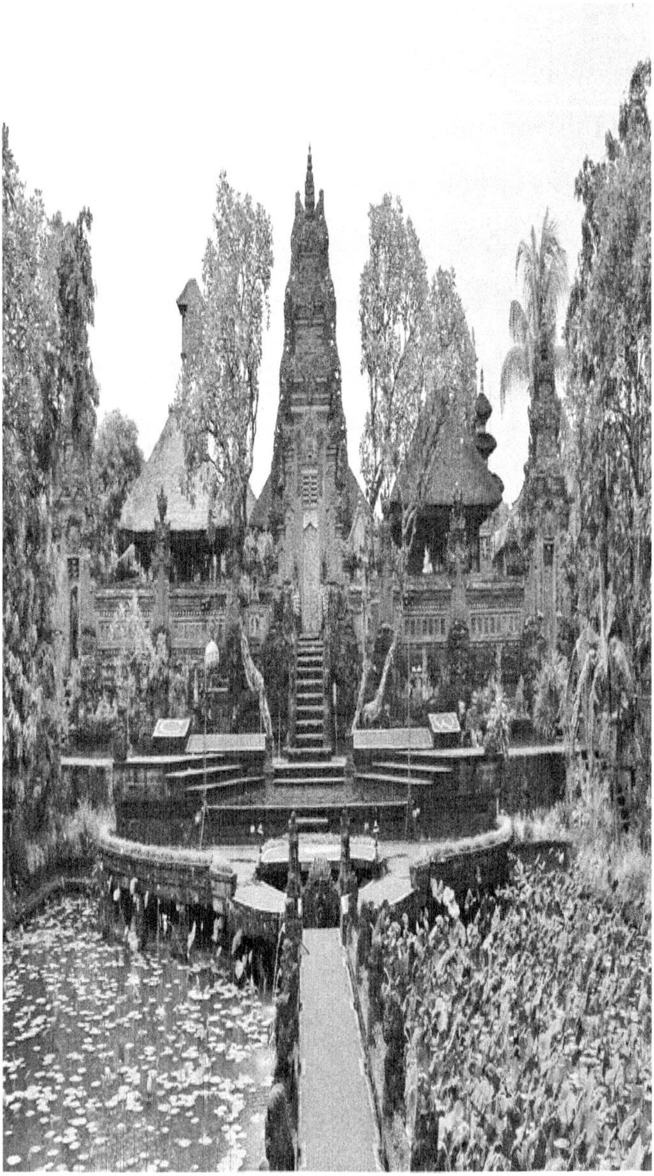

Chapter Eleven

Recommended Itineraries

One Week in Bali
One-Week Bali Itinerary

Day 1-2: Ubud – Cultural Heart of Bali

- Morning: Arrive in Bali and head to Ubud.

Check into your accommodation and explore the town.

- Afternoon: Visit the Sacred Monkey Forest Sanctuary.
- Evening: Enjoy a traditional Balinese dance performance.

Day 2:

- Morning: Explore the Tegallalang Rice Terraces.
- Afternoon: Visit the Ubud Art Market.
- Evening: Relax with a traditional Balinese massage or explore Ubud's culinary scene.

Day 3-4: South Bali – Beaches and Relaxation
- Morning: Travel to Seminyak or Canggu in South Bali.

Enjoy the beautiful beaches and check in your accommodation.
- Afternoon: Explore trendy beach clubs, shops, and cafes.
- Evening: Experience Balis nightlife with beachfront bars and clubs.

Day 4:
- Morning: Learn to surf or just unwind on the shore.
- Afternoon: Visit Tanah Lot Temple for a sunset view.
- Evening: Enjoy a seafood dinner on the beach.

Day 5-6: East Bali – Nature and Water Palaces
- Morning: Travel to East Bali and visit Tirta Gangga, a stunning water palace.

- Afternoon: Explore scenic landscapes and villages like Tenganan.
- Evening: Relax at your accommodation in East Bali.

Day 6:
- Morning: Visit Lempuyang Temple, known for its „Gates of Heaven."
- Afternoon: Explore the Ujung Water Palace.
- Evening: Enjoy a quiet dinner in the serene surroundings.

Day 7: Nusa Penida – Island Adventure
- Morning: Take a boat to Nusa Penida.
- Afternoon: Explore Kelingking Beach, Broken Beach, and Angel's Billabong.
- Evening: Return to Bali and spend your last night by the ocean.

Adjust the itinerary based on your interests and check for local events. Allow for flexibility and embrace the unique experiences Bali has to offer.

Two Weeks or More
Two-Week-Bali-Itinerary

Week 1: Exploring Cultural and Central Bali

- Day 1-3: Ubud and Surroundings
    - Day 1: Arrive in Ubud, explore the town, and visit the Sacred Monkey Forest Sanctuary.

Evening dance performance at Ubud Palace.

    - Day 2: Tegallalang Rice Terraces in the morning.

Afternoon visit to the Goa Gajah (Elephant Cave) and Tirta Empul Temple.

Evening at the Ubud Art Market.

    - Day 3: Morning trek to Campuhan Ridge Walk.

Afternoon at the Blanco Renaissance Museum.
Evening spa and relaxation.

Day 4-6: North Bali – Lovina and Surroundings

- Day 4: Travel to Lovina in North Bali.

Take a dolphin-watching tour at sunset while lounging on Lovina Beach.

- Day 5: Morning visit to Banjar Hot Springs.

Afternoon exploring the Gitgit Waterfall and surrounding area.

- Day 6: Full-day excursion to West Bali National Park and Menjangan Island for snorkeling.

Day 7-10: East Bali – Amed and Surroundings

- Day 7: Travel to Amed, known for its black sand beaches and excellent snorkeling and diving spots.

Explore local villages and enjoy a quiet evening by the sea.

- Day 8: Snorkeling or diving in Amed.

Visit the Tirta Gangga Water Palace in the afternoon.

- Day 9: Sunrise Trek to the summit of Mount Agung (if permits are available).

Relaxation in Amed.

- Day 10: Explore the traditional villages of Tenganan and Tirta Gangga.

Relax and unwind in Amed.

Week 2: South Bali and Island Hopping

- Day 11-14: South Bali and Nusa Islands
    - Day 11: Travel to the southern part of Bali (Seminyak, Canggu, or Uluwatu).

Enjoy the beaches and beach clubs.

- Day 12: Full-day exploration of Uluwatu: Uluwatu Temple, Suluban Beach, and Padang Padang Beach.

Sunset Kecak Dance at Uluwatu Temple.

- Day 13: Explore the Nusa Islands (Nusa Penida, Nusa Lembongan, and Nusa Ceningan).

Visit Kelingking Beach and Angel's Billabong on Nusa Penida.

- Day 14: Relax on the beaches of Nusa Lembongan.

Snorkeling or diving around the islands.

Return to the mainland for the evening.

Diese's two-week-itinerary provides a comprehensive experience of Bali, combining cultural exploration, nature adventures, and island hopping. Adjust the itinerary based on your interests and take advantage of the flexibility to explore additional off-the-beaten-path destinations. Remember to consider local events and ceremonies that may influence your plans.

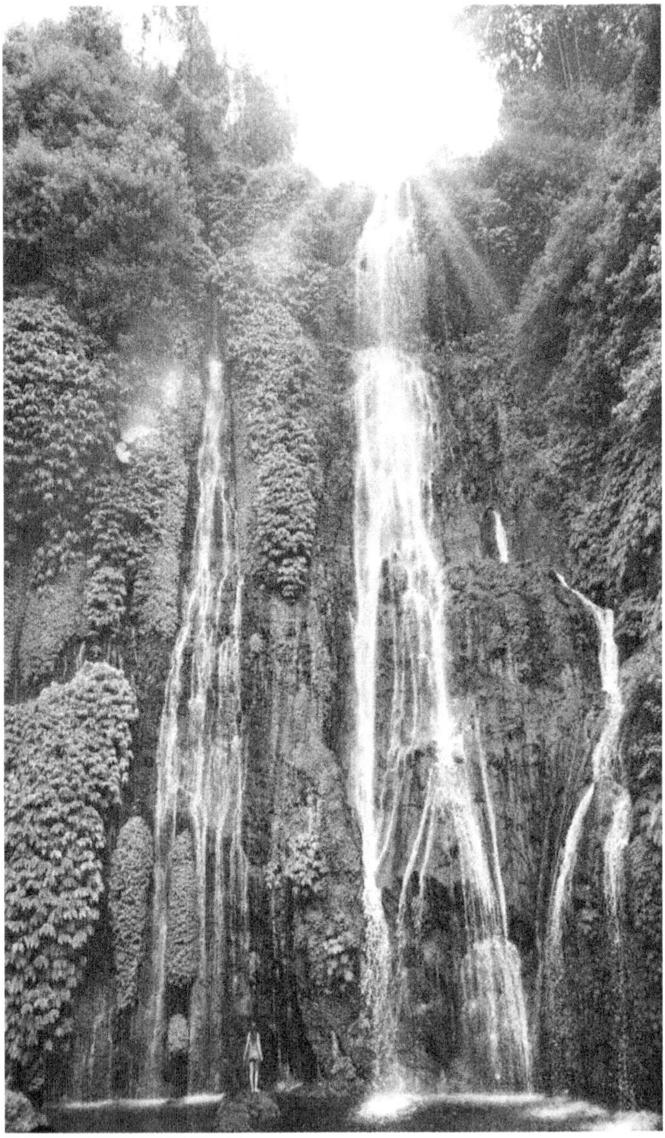

Chapter Twelve

Beyond Bali: Day Trips and Nearby Islands

Nusa Penida

Nusa Penida Itinerary

Day 1: Arrival and East Coast Exploration

- Morning: Take a boat from Sanur or Padang Bai to Nusa Penida.

Arrive at the port and check in to your accommodation.

- Afternoon: Visit Atuh Beach and Diamond Beach for stunning cliffs and clear turquoise waters.
- Evening: Enjoy the sunset at the Thousand Islands Viewpoint.

Day 2: West Coast Wonders

- Morning: Explore the iconic Kelingking Beach.

- Afternoon: Visit Angel's Billabong and Broken Beach for unique rock formations.

Relax and snorkel at Crystal Bay.

- Evening: Have a beachfront dinner with a view of the sunset.

Day 3: Central and Northern Nusa Penida

- Morning: Hike to Peguyangan Waterfall and visit the cliffside temple.
- Afternoon: Explore the lush Tembeling Forest and relax at Tembeling Beach.
- Evening: Sample local Balinese and Indonesian cuisine at a warung.

Day 4: Departure or optional activities

- Morning: Consider a snorkeling or diving excursion to explore marine life.
- Afternoon: Depending on your departure time, explore more or relax before heading back to Bali.

Tips:

Rent a scooter or hire a local driver for easier transportation.

Wear comfortable shoes for trekking and exploring.

Bring sunscreen, a hat, and plenty of water.

Be aware of tides when visiting beaches.

Nusa Penida offers a unique and adventurous experience, and this itinerary covers some of the island's most stunning locations. Adjust the schedule based on your interests and the time available.

Gili Islands

The Gili Islands Overview

Gili Trawangan:

- Activities:

Largest and most lively of the three islands.

Vibrant nightlife with beach parties, bars, and restaurants.

Popular for snorkeling and diving with numerous dive shops.

Cycling or horse-drawn carts (cidos) for transportation.

- Accommodation:

Various options from budget-friendly hostels to luxurious resorts.

- Attractions:

Sunset Point for panoramic sunset views.

For authentic street food, visit the Gili Trawangan Night Market.

Gili Air:

- Activities:

strikes a balance between Gili Trawangan and Gili Meno.

favored for diving and snorkeling among coral reefs.

Relaxed atmosphere suitable for couples and solo travelers.

Bicycles are common for transportation.

- Accommodation:

Range of options including beachfront bungalows and eco-friendly resorts.

- Attractions:

Calm beaches, local cafes, and restaurants.

Yoga classes and wellness activities.

Gili Meno:

- Activities:

Smallest and quietest of the Gili Islands.

Popular for snorkeling and diving with unique underwater sculptures.

Ideal for a peaceful retreat and romantic atmosphere.

- Accommodation:

Basic bungalows to upscale resorts, emphasizing natural beauty.

- Attractions:

Gili Meno Bird Park and Turtle Sanctuary. Pristine beaches and serene surroundings.

Getting There:

- From Bali: Fast boat or public ferry from Bali, taking 2–3 hours.
- From Lombok: Boat services available from Bangsal Harbor.

Important Tips:

- Eco-Friendly Practices: Respect the environment and support eco-friendly businesses.
- Marine Conservation: Participate in programs or tours that contribute to coral reef preservation.
- Local Culture: Dress modestly and respect local culture and traditions.

Whether seeking nightlife, a tranquil escape, or a mix of both, the Gili Islands offer diverse experiences in a stunning tropical setting.

Lombok

Lombok Itinerary: Serene Island Escape

Day 1-3: Senggigi – Beaches and Relaxation

- Day 1: Arrive in Lombok and head to Senggigi, a popular beach resort area.

Check into your accommodation and relax on the beach.

Explore the local markets and restaurants in the evening.

- Day 2: Take a boat trip to the nearby Gili Islands (Gili Trawangan, Gili Air, and Gili Meno).

Snorkel, dive, or simply enjoy the laid-back atmosphere on the islands.

- Day 3: Explore Senggigi's beautiful beaches, like Senggigi Beach and Mangsit Beach.

Visit the Pura Batu Bolong Temple for panoramic coastal views.

Savor a meal at a beachside restaurant as the sun sets.

Day 4-6: Kuta – Southern Coast Adventure

- Day 4: Travel to Kuta on the southern coast of Lombok.

Visit Kuta Beach and explore the vibrant town. Rent a scooter or hire a local guide to explore the nearby stunning beaches such as Tanjung Aan and Mawun.

- Day 5: Discover the unique culture of the Sasak people by visiting traditional Sasak villages like Sade and Rambitan.

Explore the Merese Hill for panoramic views of the coastline.

- Day 6: Take a day trip to the beautiful beaches of the southern coast, including Selong Belanak Beach and Mawi Beach.

Take pleasure in water sports like paddle boarding and surfing.

Day 7-9: Senaru – Waterfalls and Rinjani Trekking

- Day 7: Head to Senaru, the Gateway to Mount Rinjani, Lombok's highest peak.

Visit Sendang Gile and Tiu Kelep Waterfalls.

- Day 8: Embark on a trek to Mount Rinjani for a multi-day adventure. Choose a trekking package based on your preferences and fitness level.

Spend the night camping on the mountain.

- Day 9: Descend from Mount Rinjani and return to Senaru.

Relax and recover from the trek or explore the surrounding areas.

Day 10-12: Gili Islands – Island Paradise

- Day 10: Return to the Gili Islands for a more extended stay or explore a different Gili than the one you visited earlier.

Enjoy the pristine beaches and coral reefs.

- Day 11: Snorkel or dive in the crystal-clear waters surrounding the islands.

Rent a bicycle and explore the Gili Islands' charming villages.

- Day 12: Take a yoga class, have a spa treatment, or just unwind on the beach.

Enjoy a farewell dinner with a view of the sunset.

Diese's itinerary offers a mix of relaxation, adventure, and cultural exploration on the diverse and beautiful island of Lombok. Adjust the schedule based on your preferences and the time you have available, and consider local events or ceremonies that may enhance your experience.

Chapter Thirteen

Staying safe and healthy

Emergency information

Emergency Information and Safety Tips for Bali and Lombok:

Emergency Contacts:
- Medical Emergencies:
  - Ambulance: 118 or 119
  - Sanglah Hospital (Denpasar): +62 361 227911
- Police:
  - Emergency Police Number: 110
- Tourist Police:
  - Bali Tourist Police: +62 361 754599
- Fire Department:
  - Emergency Fire Number: 113
- Search and Rescue:
  - Basarnas (National Search and Rescue Agency): 115

General Safety Tips:

- Travel Insurance:

Make sure you have comprehensive travel insurance that covers cancellations due to illness.

- Health Precautions:

Stay hydrated, use sunscreen, mosquito repellent, and take necessary vaccinations.

Local Laws and Customs:

Learn about the laws, traditions, and customs of the area.

- Safe Transportation:

Use reputable transportation services and wear helmets on scooters.

- Emergency Funds:

Keep a small amount of local currency and emergency credit or cash.

- Natural Disasters:

Be aware of local weather conditions and follow guidance during emergencies

- Water Safety:

Be cautious of strong currents, swim in designated areas, and follow lifeguard guidelines.

- Tour Operator Safety:

Choose reputable operators following safety standards for excursions.

- Cultural Sensitivity:

Respect local customs, dress modestly at temples, and remove shoes when required.

- Document copies:

Keep copies of important documents in a separate location.

- Local Currency:

Carry small denominations of local currency for small purchases and tips.

- Emergency Kit:

Pack a small kit with first aid supplies, medications, and important contacts.

- Communication:

Use international roaming or a local SIM card for communication.

- Stay informed:

Stay updated on local news, travel advisories, and register with your embassy.

Remember, Bali and Lombok are generally safe, but being prepared and informed ensures a smooth trip. Exercise caution, trust your instincts, and seek assistance if needed.

Health Precautions

Ensuring good health during your trip to Bali or Lombok involves taking certain precautions to prevent common travel-related health issues. Here are some health precautions and tips for a safe and healthy journey:

- Vaccinations:

Check with your healthcare provider about recommended and required vaccinations for Indonesia. Routine vaccines such as measles, mumps, rubella (MMR), diphtheria, tetanus, and pertussis (DTP) should be up to date. Hepatitis A and B, typhoid, and Japanese encephalitis vaccines may also be recommended.

- Mosquito-Borne Diseases:

Malaria is present in some parts of Indonesia, including rural areas of Lombok. Consult your healthcare provider about antimalarial medications. Use mosquito repellent, wear long sleeves, and sleep under a mosquito net, especially in high-risk areas.

- Food and Water Safety:

Stick to bottled or boiled water and avoid consuming ice in drinks. Be cautious about consuming raw or undercooked seafood and meats. Choose food from reputable and hygienic establishments. Always bring hand sanitizer with you and wash your hands often.

- Sun Protection:

Bali and Lombok have a tropical climate, and Sun exposure can be intense. Use sunscreen with a high SPF, wear a hat, sunglasses and protective clothing. Stay hydrated to prevent heat-related Illnesses.

- Hydration:

Drink plenty of water, especially in the tropical climate. Dehydration can lead to various health issues, so carry a reusable water bottle and refill it regularly.

- Travelers Diarrhea:

Be cautious about street food and uncooked or undercooked dishes. Wash your hands before eating, and consider using probiotics to support digestive health. Pack over-the-counter medications for diarrhea and other stomach issues.

- Motion Sickness:

If you plan to travel on boats or winding roads, consider bringing motion sickness medication, if you're prone to seasickness or motion-related discomfort.

- Health Insurance:

Ensure you have comprehensive travel insurance that covers medical emergencies and evacuation. Become familiar with the policies and processes for handling emergencies.

- Medical Kit:

Pack a small medical kit with essentials such as pain relievers, antidiarrheal medications, adhesive bandages, antiseptic wipes, and any prescription medications you may need.

- Local Health Facilities:

Identify reputable hospitals and clinics in the areas you will be visiting. In Bali, Sanglah Hospital in Denpasar is a major medical facility. In Lombok, the main hospital is Rumah Sakit Umum Kota Mataram.

- Air Quality:

In certain months, particularly during the dry season, haze from forest fires may affect air quality. If you have respiratory issues, monitor air quality and consider wearing a mask if necessary.

- Stay active:

Stay physically active to boost your immune system and overall well-being. Engage in outdoor activities but be mindful of your limits, especially in the heat.

- Animal Bites:

Avoid contact with stray animals, as rabies is present in some parts of Indonesia. If bitten or scratched, seek immediate medical attention.

Before your trip, consult with a travel-health-specialist or your healthcare provider to discuss specific health precautions based on your individual needs and health history. Taking these precautions can contribute to a healthy and enjoyable travel experience in Bali and Lombok.

Travel Insurance

Having comprehensive travel insurance is a crucial aspect of trip planning. In the event of unforeseen circumstances, it offers peace of mind and financial security.

Here are some key considerations and tips for obtaining travel insurance for your trip to Bali or Lombok:

- Coverage:

Ensure your travel insurance covers a wide range of aspects, including medical emergencies, trip cancellations or interruptions, lost or stolen belongings, and emergency evacuation.

- Medical Coverage:

Verify that the insurance provides sufficient coverage for medical expenses, including hospital stays, medications, and emergency medical evacuation. Some countries may require upfront payment for medical services, so having coverage that pays directly to the healthcare provider can be beneficial.

- Adventure Activities:

If you plan to engage in adventure activities such as diving, trekking, or watersports, confirm that your insurance covers these activities. Some insurers have exclusions for certain high-risk activities.

- Trip Cancellations:

Check the policy's coverage for trip cancellations or interruptions due to unforeseen circumstances such as illness, family emergencies, or unexpected changes in travel plans.

- Baggage and Belongings:

Ensure your insurance covers the loss, theft, or damage to your baggage and personal belongings. It's helpful to document valuable items before the trip and keep receipts for expensive items.

- Travel Delays:

Confirm coverage for travel delays, missed connections, and additional expenses incurred due to unforeseen delays.

- Emergency Assistance Services:

Look for insurance that provides 24/7 emergency assistance services. Dieses can be crucial, in case you need help navigating a medical emergency, locating medical facilities, or coordinating evacuations.

- Pre-existing conditions:

Disclose any pre-existing medical conditions when purchasing insurance. Pre-existing conditions may not be covered by certain insurance, or they may need higher premiums.

- Policy Limits and Exclusions:

Understand the policy limits, deductibles, and exclusions. Pay attention to coverage limits for medical expenses, evacuation costs, and the overall policy maximum.

- Length of Coverage:

Ensure the insurance covers the entire duration of your trip, including any planned extensions. Some policies have a maximum trip duration, so choose one that aligns with your travel plans.

- Review and Compare Policies:

Before purchasing insurance, carefully review the terms and conditions of different policies. Compare coverage, costs, and customer reviews to choose the one that best meets your needs.

- Purchase early:

It's advisable to purchase travel insurance as soon as you book your trip. Some benefits, such as trip cancellation coverage, may only apply if the insurance is purchased within a certain time frame after booking.

- Keep a copy:

Carry a copy of your insurance policy, emergency contact numbers, and any relevant information with you during your trip.

By taking the time to choose the right travel insurance policy and understanding its terms, you can better protect yourself from unexpected situations and focus on enjoying your time in Bali or Lombok.

Conclusion

As the final chapter unfolds in our Bali Travel Guide 2024, it marks the culmination of a journey through a realm that transcends the confines of a typical tropical paradise. Bali, with its rich tapestry of culture, vibrant landscapes, and warm hospitality, has provided an immersive experience that extends beyond the pages of this guidebook. As we conclude this exploration, let us reflect on the enchanting tapestry of Bali, weaving together its diverse facets into a captivating mosaic that beckons travelers from across the globe.

Balis allure lies not only in its pristine beaches and lush landscapes, but also in the cultural symphony that plays out across its villages and temples. The island's soul resonates with a harmonious blend of tradition and modernity, where ancient rituals and customs coexist with contemporary influences. Exploring the sacred temples, such as Uluwatu and Tanah Lot, one cannot help but feel the spiritual pulse that beats through the heart of Bali. The intricate dance of Kecak, the melodious Gamelan music, and the vibrant festivals reveal a cultural richness that is both captivating and timeless.

The guide has navigated readers through the diverse landscapes of Bali, each offering a unique palette of experiences. From the emerald rice terraces of Tegallalang to the majestic Mount Batur, Bali unfolds its natural wonders in a breathtaking panorama. The tranquil waters of Gitgit Waterfall and the vibrant marine life around Menjangan Island beckon adventure seekers and nature enthusiasts alike. The conclusion of this guide invites us to savor the beauty of Bali's nature, encouraging us to immerse ourselves in the island's serene tranquility.

Culinary delights have played a significant role in our journey, and the guide has been a compass leading us to the finest dining experiences Bali has to offer. From the bustling street food stalls to the upscale beachfront restaurants, the island's cuisine is a sensory journey. The aromatic spices, fresh seafood, and tropical fruits have tantalized our taste buds, creating a culinary adventure that mirrors Balis diversity and authenticity.

The exploration of Bali in 2024 has also unveiled the island's commitment to sustainable tourism. The guide has emphasized responsible travel practices, encouraging readers to engage with local communities and support eco-friendly initiatives. Bali's dedication to preserving its natural and cultural heritage is evident in initiatives like beach clean-ups, organic farming, and community-based tourism projects. The conclusion of this guide serves as a reminder that responsible tourism is not just an option, but an imperative for the preservation of Bali's beauty for future generations.

In closing, Bali is more than just a destination; It is an experience that lingers in the hearts of those fortunate enough to tread its shores. The Bali Travel Guide 2024 has endeavored to capture the essence of this magical island, offering a glimpse into its soul. As we bid farewell to these pages, may the memories created and the insights gained serve as a compass for future journeys. Bali, with its ever-evolving tapestry, remains an eternal invitation, beckoning travelers to uncover the treasures that await on this enchanting island. Until we meet again in the embrace of Balis warmth and beauty, let this guide be a testament to the timeless allure of the Island of the Gods.